HOOKED ON AMIGURUMI

HOOKED ON
AMIGURUMI

40 Fun Patterns for Playful Crochet Plushes

MELANIE MORITA
Founder of Knot Too Shabby Crochet

PAGE STREET
PUBLISHING CO.

PAGE STREET
PUBLISHING CO.

First published in 2019 by

Page Street Publishing Co.

27 Congress Street, Suite 105

Salem, MA 01970

www.pagestreetpublishing.com

Distributed by Macmillan, sales in Canada by The Canadian Manda Group.

23 22 21 20 19   3 4 5

ISBN-13: 978-1-62414-766-1

ISBN-10: 1-62414-766-6

Library of Congress Control Number: 2018957263

Cover and book design by Rosie Stewart for Page Street Publishing Co.

Photography by Melanie Morita

Printed and bound in China

TO MY FELLOW CREATIVE BOSS BABES:
YOUR STRENGTH, CREATIVITY AND
DEDICATION TRULY INSPIRE ME.

AND

TO MY AMAZING FIANCÉ, DAVID:
THANK YOU FOR YOUR ENDLESS SUPPORT.
I CAN'T WAIT TO SPEND FOREVER WITH YOU.

TABLE OF CONTENTS

INTRODUCTION

Amigurumi is the Japanese word for knitted or crocheted stuffed toys, and it is such a fun and beautiful craft. The fact that you can create absolutely anything from just a bit of yarn and a hook still astounds me. Crochet isn't just about granny squares and scarves anymore—the possibilities are truly endless!

This book focuses on using unique techniques and skills to minimize sewing and create beautiful seamless pieces. I will take you step by step through 40 of my favorite designs using a wide variety of styles and methods to challenge and inspire you.

Amigurumi is typically worked in spiral rounds and starts with a small ring of stitches. Then a series of increasing and decreasing stitches build upon each other to give your piece shape and dimension. Typically, you'd have to complete the main body, then attach the extra limbs by sewing. This can often be very tedious and finicky! Thus began my endeavor to find an easier, faster solution.

My journey started with a little birdie plush I made in college—halfway through a bottle of wine, during girl's night in. From then on, I was hooked (pun intended)! After making my first couple of creations, I quickly realized that sewing just wasn't for me, so I started to develop my own designs, techniques and unique style.

Five years later, I started my Knot Too Shabby Crochet Etsy shop in secret. There were only two items listed, but just a couple of weeks later I made my first sale. After that, I dove in head first. I picked up a camera and my crochet hook, and

I got to work! As my business grew, there were countless challenges and learning experiences along the way. But I am incredibly thankful to have had the opportunity to partake in some amazing experiences: from attending craft fairs, to participating in fun collaborations, and even writing this book!

As you peek through the book, you'll notice that it's organized into chapters based on theme: Beach Bums (page 11), Once Upon a Time (page 35), Eat Your Heart Out (page 61), Bento Box (page 95) and Sip Sip Hooray (page 117). Each chapter includes projects of varying levels of difficulty, ranging in skill from 1 (easiest) to 5 (hardest). Those with some experience are welcome to dive right in. But for beginners, I recommend looking through the chapters and working on some of the easier patterns to get warmed up. When you have a good handle on the basics, try out some of the more advanced projects, or use some of the techniques you learned to add some style! If you are new to crochet or need a refresher, check out the back of the book (page 137) for a crash course in all things amigurumi. I share my favorite supplies and cover some of the basics to get you started.

The patterns in this book are bright, colorful, fun and designed specifically to keep sewing to a minimum. The big personalities and adorable blushing faces truly bring each design to life. They make the perfect gift, ornament, keychain or décor item for all ages. I hope they bring you and your loved ones lots of cheer and joy! Happy crocheting!

BEACH BUMS

Crochet can provide a much-needed escape from the chaos of the day. Just pick up your hook and let the dirty laundry, unwashed dishes and crazy kids/pups fade away. Relax as you are transported to a warm, sunny beach with the wind in your hair, the sand between your toes and the soothing sound of the ocean waves crashing in the distance.

This chapter is filled with all the water-loving creatures and beachy vibes of the perfect tropical escape from reality. The whimsical jellyfish (page 19), mysterious whale (page 27) and majestic sea turtle (page 13) are bright, cheery and full of love. They will leave you smiling and ready to take on the day!

For me, those little moments of crochet therapy scattered throughout the week help me to keep my sanity. There never seems to be enough hours in the day for everything—between working full time, managing my side business and caring for my wild and crazy fur babies (aka puppies). We've all been there—life is either sink or swim! But for now, kick up your feet, take your time and enjoy the moment. I won't leave you high and dry much longer. Let's dive in!

SHELLY
the Sea Turtle

Say hello to Shelly the Sea Turtle. Even though she looks tough with her strong protective shell, she's actually quite shy. But once you coax her out of her shell, you'll realize just how sweet she is. Shelly the Sea Turtle is worked in continuous rounds and joins together with no sewing necessary. The fins start as circles and are then folded in half to give them shape. The head, fins and tail are then worked into the body. Shelly swims about 2.5 inches (6.5 cm) tall and 6 inches (15.5 cm) long.

FRONT FINS

This piece starts at the center of each fin using green yarn. Repeat the pattern so you have two fins.

R1: 8 sc in MR (8)

R2: 1 inc in each st (16)

R3: [1 sc, 1 inc] x8 (24)

R4: [2 sc, 1 inc] x8 (32)

Fold the piece in half.

R5: Ch 1, then, working through the front and back stitches, sc 16 (16)

Ch 1 then fasten off. No need to weave in the ends, the yarn will end up inside the piece.

Front fins, round 5

(CONTINUED)

MATERIALS

1 oz green worsted weight/4-ply yarn

1 oz golden-brown worsted weight/4-ply yarn

0.5 oz tan worsted weight/4-ply yarn

Size E-4 (3.5 mm) crochet hook

Stitch markers

2 (6-mm) black plastic safety eyes

Polyester fiberfill

Tapestry needle

TERMINOLOGY

R1:	row 1 or round 1
st(s):	stitch(es)
slst:	slip stitch
ch:	chain
sc:	single crochet
inc:	single crochet increase
dec:	invisible decrease
MR:	magic ring
FLO:	front loops only

Shelly the Sea Turtle (Continued)

BACK FINS

This piece starts at the center of each fin using green yarn. Repeat the pattern so you have two fins.

R1: 6 sc in MR (6)

R2: 1 inc in each st (12)

R3: [1 sc, 1 inc] x6 (18)

Fold the piece in half.

R4: Ch 1, then, working through the front and back stitches, sc 9 (9)

Ch 1 then fasten off. No need to weave in the ends, the yarn will end up inside the piece.

HEAD

This piece starts at the front of the head using green yarn.

R1: 6 sc in MR (6)

R2: 1 inc in each st (12)

R3: [1 sc, 1 inc] x6 (18)

R4: 2 sc, 1 inc, 2 sc, 1 inc. Place a stitch marker on st 8 to mark a space for the eyes. 2 sc, 1 inc, 2 sc, 1 inc, 2 sc, 1 inc. Place a stitch marker on st 20 to mark a space for the eyes. 2 sc, 1 inc (24)

R5-8: 1 sc in each st (24)

Place the eyes between R4 and R5 where you placed your stitch markers.

R9: [2 sc, 1 dec] x6 (18)

R10: [1 sc, 1 dec] x6 (12)

R11: 6 dec (6)

Stuff the piece with polyester fiberfill and flatten.

R12: Ch 1, turn, then, working through the front and back stitches, sc 3 (3)

Ch 1 then fasten off. No need to weave in the ends, the yarn will end up inside the piece.

TAIL

This piece starts at the tip of the tail using green yarn.

R1: 4 sc in MR (4)

R2: [1 sc, 1 inc] x2 (6)

Flatten the piece.

R3: Ch 1, turn, then working through the front and back stitches, sc 3 (3)

Ch 1 then fasten off. No need to weave in the ends, the yarn will end up inside the piece.

SHELL

This piece starts at the top of the shell using golden-brown yarn.

R1: 6 sc in MR (6)

R2: 1 inc in each st (12)

R3: [1 sc, 1 inc] x6 (18)

R4: [2 sc, 1 inc] x6 (24)

R5: [3 sc, 1 inc] x6 (30)

R6: [4 sc, 1 inc] x6 (36)

R7-10: 1 sc in each st (36)

R11: Working in FLO, [5 sc, 1 inc] x6 (42)

Slst in next st. Fasten off, and then weave in the ends with a tapestry needle.

(CONTINUED)

Back fins, round 4

Head, fasten off

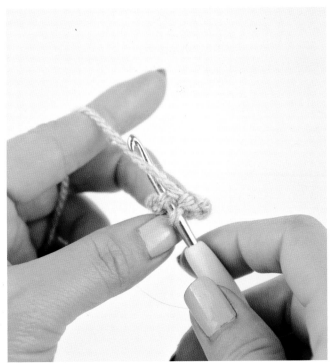

Tail, round 1

Shell, finished

Shelly the Sea Turtle (Continued)

BELLY

Using tan yarn, join the yarn to the first back loop from R11 of the shell.

In the next round, we will attach the head, fins and tail by working through the body and each piece simultaneously. Line up each piece as shown.

R1: 2 sc, then, working through the tail and belly, sc 3. 2 sc, then, working through the back fin and belly, sc 2. 5 sc, then, working through the front fin and belly, sc 3. 3 sc, then, working through the head and belly, sc 3. 3 sc, then, working through the front fin and belly, 3 sc. 5 sc, then, working through the back fin and belly, sc 2. (36)

R1: [4 sc, 1 dec] x6 (30)

R2: [3 sc, 1 dec] x6 (24)

R3: [2 sc, 1 dec] x6 (18)

R4: [1 sc, 1 dec] x6 (12)

R5: 6 dec (6)

Stuff the piece with polyester fiberfill. Close off, and then weave in the ends with a tapestry needle.

Belly, joining yarn

Belly, joining fins

Belly, finished

Shelly the Sea Turtle, finished

Jilly
the Jellyfish

Jellyfish love to float and bob through the ocean without a care in the world. But not Jilly, she is totally spineless and terrified of the ocean! She would much rather hang out somewhere high where she can dance and sway the night away. Jilly the Jellyfish is worked in continuous rounds. The pattern starts with the body, leaving a round of free loops to attach the belly. Then each tentacle is attached to the bottom of the belly. This pattern calls for pink yarn, but feel free to personalize your jellyfish! Hang her up somewhere high and watch her little tentacles sway. Jilly's body is approximately 2 inches (5 cm) tall, and her tentacles are about 5 inches (13 cm) long but can be made to any length.

BODY

The piece starts at the top of the body using pink yarn.

R1: 6 sc in MR (6)

R2: 1 inc in each st (12)

R3: [1 sc, 1 inc] x6 (18)

R4: [2 sc, 1 inc] x6 (24)

R5: [3 sc, 1 inc] x6 (30)

R6: [4 sc, 1 inc] x6 (36)

R7–12: 1 sc in each st (36)

R13: [4 sc, 1 dec] x6 (30)

Place the eyes between R11 and R12, about 4 sc apart. Using black yarn, embroider the mouth onto the front of the face with the tapestry needle, just below the eyes. Add blush for rosy pink cheeks, if you'd like.

R14: Working in FLO, [1 slst, 3 hdc in the next st] x15 (60)

Slst in next st. Fasten off and weave in the ends with the tapestry needle.

Body, finished

(CONTINUED)

MATERIALS

1.5 oz pink worsted weight/4-ply yarn

Size E-4 (3.5 mm) crochet hook

Stitch markers

2 (6-mm) black plastic safety eyes

Scrap piece of black yarn for embroidery

Tapestry needle

Cosmetic blush, for adding cheeks (optional)

Polyester fiberfill

TERMINOLOGY

R1:	row 1 or round 1
st(s):	stitch(es)
slst:	slip stitch
ch:	chain
sc:	single crochet
hdc:	half double crochet
inc:	single crochet increase
dec:	invisible decrease
sc2tog:	single crochet two together
MR:	magic ring
FLO:	front loops only

Jilly the Jellyfish (Continued)

BELLY

Using pink yarn, join the yarn to the first back loop from R14 of the body.

R1: [3 sc, 1 sc2tog] x6 (24)

R2: [2 sc, 1 dec] x6 (18)

R3: [1 sc, 1 dec] x6 (12)

R4: 6 dec (6)

Stuff the piece with the polyester fiberfill. Close off, and then weave in the ends with the tapestry needle.

THIN TENTACLES

Use pink yarn for this piece and repeat the pattern until you have five tentacles.

Ch 25 (25)

Fasten off. Use the excess yarn ends to attach each tentacle to the body at the center of the belly, as shown. Weave in the ends with the tapestry needle.

CURLY TENTACLES

Use pink yarn for this piece, and repeat the pattern until you have five tentacles.

Ch 31 to create a foundation chain. Starting at the second chain from hook, [1sc, 1 inc] x15 (45)

Fasten off. Use the excess yarn ends to attach each tentacle to the bottom of the body along the outside edge, as shown. Weave in the ends with the tapestry needle.

Belly, joining yarn

Belly, finished

Thin tentacles, finished

Curly tentacles, finished

Jilly the Jellyfish, finished

Inky

the Octopus

Some days you just need an extra set of arms (or four) to get you through your never-ending to-do list. Well, Inky the Octopus has got you covered. His little tentacles may be stumpy, but don't let that fool you. He is a force to be reckoned with! Inky the Octopus is worked in continuous rounds and requires no sewing. The tentacles are made first and worked into the body. This pattern calls for purple yarn, but feel free to personalize your octopus! Inky's finished size is approximately 5 inches (13 cm) tall and 5 inches (13 cm) long.

TENTACLES

This piece starts at the tip of each tentacle using light purple yarn. Repeat the pattern until you have eight tentacles.

R1: 6 sc in MR (6)

R2: 1 inc in each st (12)

R3–5: 1 sc in each st (12)

R6: [2 sc, 1 dec] x3 (9)

R7: 1 sc in each st (9)

R8: [1 sc, 1 dec] x3 (6)

Stuff the piece with the polyester fiberfill and flatten the opening.

R9: Ch 1, turn, then working through the front and back stitches, sc 3 (3)

Ch 1 then fasten off. No need to weave in the ends, the yarn will end up inside the piece.

Tentacle, finished

(CONTINUED)

(CONTINUED)

SKILL LEVEL

MATERIALS

2 oz light purple worsted weight/ 4-ply yarn

Size E-4 (3.5 mm) crochet hook

Stitch markers

2 (6-mm) black plastic safety eyes

Scrap piece of black yarn for embroidery

Polyester fiberfill

Tapestry needle

Cosmetic blush, for adding cheeks (optional)

TERMINOLOGY

R1:	row 1 or round 1
st(s):	stitch(es)
ch:	chain
sc:	single crochet
inc:	single crochet increase
dec:	invisible decrease
MR:	magic ring

Inky the Octopus (Continued)

HEAD

This piece starts at the top of the head using light purple yarn.

R1: 6 sc in MR (6)

R2: 1 inc in each st (12)

R3: [1 sc, 1 inc] x6 (18)

R4: [2 sc, 1 inc] x6 (24)

R5: [3 sc, 1 inc] x6 (30)

R6: [4 sc, 1 inc] x6 (36)

R7: [5 sc, 1 inc] x6 (42)

R8: [6 sc, 1 inc] x6 (48)

R9–16: 1 sc in each st (48)

R17: [6 sc, 1 dec] x6 (42)

R18: [5 sc, 1 dec] x6 (36)

R19: [4 sc, 1 dec] x6 (30)

R20: [3 sc, 1 dec] x6 (24)

Head, round 21

Place the eyes between R15 and R16, about 6 sc apart. Using black yarn, embroider the mouth onto the front of the face with the tapestry needle, just below the eyes. Add blush for rosy pink cheeks, if you'd like.

In the next round, we will attach the tentacles by working through head and tentacles simultaneously.

R21: [Working through the body and one tentacle at a time, sc 3] x8 (24)

R22: [2 sc, 1 dec] x6 (18)

R23: [1 sc, 1 dec] x6 (12)

R24: 6 dec (6)

Stuff the piece with the polyester fiberfill. Close off, and then weave in the ends with the tapestry needle.

Inky the Octopus, finished

STARLA
the Starfish

While I was in school, one of my favorite getaways was this secluded little beach tucked behind a quiet neighborhood in Orange County. I could explore those tide pools for hours, each little crevice hiding a mysterious anemone or twinkling starfish. This pattern perfectly encapsulates those magical memories. Starla the Starfish is worked in continuous rounds and joins together with no sewing necessary. The starfish starts with a magic ring, then a series of chains is formed to give shape to each leg. The front and back pieces are joined by working through both simultaneously to close. Starla's finished size is approximately 4.5 inches (11.5 cm) tall and 4.5 inches (11.5 cm) wide.

STAR

Repeat this pattern to create Starla's front and back pieces. Each piece starts at the center of the starfish and works outward using orange yarn.

R1: 5 sc in MR (5)

In the next round, we will use a series of chains to create each leg.

R2: [1 sc, ch 7, then, starting at the second chain from the hook, 6 sc in the back loops of the ch, 1 sc in the starting st] x5 (70)

R3: [1 sc2tog, 4 sc, 2 inc, 4 sc, 1 sc2tog] x5 (70)

Slst in next st and fasten off.

On one piece, place the eyes between R2 and R3, on each side of the face. Using black yarn, embroider the mouth onto the front of the face with the tapestry needle, just below the eyes.

FINISHING

Line up the two stars with the correct side of the stitches facing outward. Using orange yarn, insert the crochet hook through ch1 in both pieces to join. Work through both pieces simultaneously and stuff periodically with fiberfill.

R1: 1 sc in each st to close (70)

Slst in next st. Fasten off and weave in the ends with a tapestry needle.

Finishing, round 1

MATERIALS

1 oz orange worsted weight/4-ply yarn

Size E-4 (3.5 mm) crochet hook

Stitch markers

2 (6-mm) black plastic safety eyes

Scrap piece of black yarn for embroidery

Polyester fiberfill

Tapestry needle

TERMINOLOGY

R1:	row 1 or round 1
st(s):	stitch(es)
slst:	slip stitch
ch:	chain
sc:	single crochet
inc:	single crochet increase
dec:	invisible decrease
sc2tog:	single crochet two together
MR:	magic ring

WiLLy
the Whale

When life has you feeling like a fish out of water, Willy the Whale is here to help you through it. Cuddle up with this cutie and everything whale be just fine. Willy the Whale is worked in continuous rounds and joins together with no sewing necessary. Each side of the tail is made separately and joined together to create a seamless piece. Then the fins and tail are worked into the main body to avoid the hassle of sewing. This pattern calls for blue and white yarn, but feel free to personalize your whale! Willy swims at approximately 3 inches (8 cm) tall and 4.5 inches (11.5 cm) long.

FINS

This piece starts at the tip of each fin using light blue yarn. Repeat the pattern so you have two fins.

R1: 6 sc in MR (6)

R2: 1 inc in each st (12)

R3: 1 sc in each st (12)

R4: 1 sc in each st (12)

Flatten the piece.

R5: Ch 1, turn, then working through the front and back stitches, sc 6 (6)

Ch 1 then fasten off. No need to weave in the ends, the yarn will end up inside the piece.

TAIL PART 1

This piece starts at the tip of the first part of the tail using light blue yarn.

R1: 4 sc in MR (4)

R2: [1 sc, 1 inc] x2 (6)

R3: [1 sc, 1 inc] x3 (9)

R4: [2 sc, 1 inc] x3 (12)

R5: [2 sc, 1 dec] x3 (9)

Slst in next st and fasten off.

Fins, round 5

Tail part 2, joining

(CONTINUED)

MATERIALS

1 oz light blue worsted weight/ 4-ply yarn

0.5 oz white worsted weight/4-ply yarn

Size E-4 (3.5 mm) crochet hook

Stitch markers

2 (6-mm) black plastic safety eyes

Scrap piece of black yarn for embroidery

Polyester fiberfill

Tapestry needle

TERMINOLOGY

R1:	row 1 or round 1
st(s):	stitch(es)
slst:	slip stitch
ch:	chain
sc:	single crochet
inc:	single crochet increase
dec:	invisible decrease
sc2tog:	single crochet two together
MR:	magic ring
BLO:	back loops only

Willy the Whale (Continued)

TAIL PART 2

This piece starts at the tip of the second part of the tail using light blue yarn.

R1: 4 sc in MR (4)

R2: [1 sc, 1 inc] x2 (6)

R3: [1 sc, 1 inc] x3 (9)

R4: [2 sc, 1 inc] x3 (12)

R5: [2 sc, 1 dec] x3 (9)

Hold the tail sections together as shown. With the last loop of the tail piece still on your hook, slst 1 through both pieces to join. To begin the next round, start by crocheting clockwise around both pieces, excluding the slst used to join.

R6: 2 sc, 2 dec, 4 sc, 2 dec, 2 sc (12)

After R6, work 3 sc so the yarn end lines up with the side of the tail. Flatten the piece.

R7: Ch 1, turn, then working through the front and back stitches, sc 6 (6)

Ch 1 then fasten off. No need to weave in the ends, the yarn will end up inside the piece.

BODY

This piece starts at the top of the body using light blue yarn.

R1: 6 sc in MR (6)

R2: 1 inc in each st (12)

R3: [1 sc, 1 inc] x6 (18)

R4: [2 sc, 1 inc] x6 (24)

R5: [3 sc, 1 inc] x6 (30)

R6: [4 sc, 1 inc] x6 (36)

R7: 31 sc, 1 inc, 4 sc (37)

R8: 32 sc, 1 inc, 4 sc (38)

R9: 33 sc, 1 inc, 4 sc (39)

R10: 34 sc, 1 inc, 4 sc (40)

R11: 35 sc, 1 inc, 4 sc (41)

R12: 36 sc, 1 inc, 4 sc (42)

In the next round, we will attach the fins and tail by working through the body and each piece simultaneously.

R13: 4 sc, then, working through one fin and the body, 6 sc. 12 sc, then, working through the second fin and the body, 6 sc. 6 sc, then, working through the tail and body, sc 6. 2 sc (42)

Place the eyes between R11 and R12, about 10 sc apart.

Switch to white yarn.

R14: Working in BLO, [4 sc, 1 sc2tog] x7 (35)

R15: [3 sc, 1 dec] x7 (28)

R16: [2 sc, 1 dec] x7 (21)

R17: [1 sc, 1 dec] x7 (14)

R18: 7 dec (7)

Stuff the piece with polyester fiberfill. Close off, and then weave in the ends with a tapestry needle.

Tail, finished

Body, round 13

Willy the Whale, finished

CLAUDIA
the Crab

When you first meet Claudia the Crab, she can be a bit snippy. But once you get to know her, she is a true friend. If you ever find yourself in hot water, she will be there for you in a pinch! Claudia the Crab is worked in continuous rounds and joins together with no sewing necessary. The tips of the claws are made first and joined together to complete a seamless pair. Once the legs and claws are completed, they are worked into the body. Claudia stands about 2.5 inches (6.5 cm) tall and 6 inches (15.5 cm) wide.

LEGS

This piece starts at the tip of each leg. Repeat the pattern until you have six legs.

R1: 6 sc in MR (6)

R2: 1 sc in each st (6)

R3: 1 sc in each st (6)

R4: 2 inc, 2 dec (6)

R5: 1 sc in each st (6)

R6: 1 sc in each st (6)

Stuff the piece with polyester fiberfill and flatten the opening.

R7: Ch 1, turn, then, working through the front and back stitches, sc 3 (3)

Ch 1 then fasten off. No need to weave in the ends, the yarn will end up inside the piece. The legs should have a slight natural bend.

Leg, finished

(CONTINUED)

MATERIALS

2 oz red worsted weight/4-ply yarn

Size E-4 (3.5 mm) crochet hook

Stitch markers

2 (6-mm) black plastic safety eyes

Scrap piece of black yarn for embroidery

Polyester fiberfill

Tapestry needle

TERMINOLOGY

R1:	row 1 or round 1
st(s):	stitch(es)
slst:	slip stitch
ch:	chain
sc:	single crochet
inc:	single crochet increase
dec:	invisible decrease
MR:	magic ring
FLO:	front loops only

Claudia the Crab (Continued)

CLAWS

Each claw is broken up into three components. The thumb and point are made first then joined together and continued to finish the arm. Repeat this pattern so you have two claws.

THUMB

This piece starts at the tip of the thumb.

R1: 4 sc in MR (4)

R2: [1 sc, 1 inc] x2 (6)

Slst in next st and fasten off.

POINT

This piece starts at the tip of the point.

R1: 4 sc in MR (4)

R2: [1 sc, 1 inc] x2 (6)

R3: [1 sc, 1 inc] x3 (9)

R4: [2 sc, 1 inc] x3 (12)

Leave your hook in the last stitch and proceed to the arm.

ARM

Thumb and point the claw sections together as shown. With the last loop of the point piece still on your hook, slst 1 through both pieces to join. To begin the next round, start by crocheting clockwise around both pieces, excluding the slst used to join.

R1: 1 sc in each st (16)

R2: [2 sc, 1 dec] x4 (12)

Stuff the piece with polyester fiberfill.

R3: 6 dec (6)

R4–6: 1 sc in each st (6)

Work 1 sc so the yarn end lines up with the side of the claw

Stuff the piece with polyester fiberfill and flatten the opening.

R7: Ch 1, turn, then, working through the front and back stitches, sc 3 (3)

Ch 1 then fasten off. No need to weave in the ends, the yarn will end up inside the piece.

(CONTINUED)

Arm, joining

Arm, finished

Claudia the Crab (Continued)

BODY

This piece starts at the top of the body using a foundation chain to create an oval.

R1: Ch 5 to create a foundation chain. Starting at the second chain from the hook, sc 3 in the back loops of the foundation chain. 1 inc in the last stitch, rotate the chain, then 1 sc in the front loop of the same stitch. 2 sc in the front loops, 1 inc in the last stitch (10)

R2: 1 inc, 2 sc, 3 inc, 2 sc, 2 inc (16)

R3: 1 sc, 1 inc, 3 sc, 1 inc, 1 sc, 1 inc, 1 sc, 1 inc, 3 sc, 1 inc, 1 sc, 1 inc (22)

R4: 2 sc, 1 inc, 4 sc, 1 inc, 2 sc, 1 inc, 2 sc, 1 inc, 4 sc, 1 inc, 2 sc, 1 inc (28)

R5: 3 sc, 1 inc, 5 sc, 1 inc, 3 sc, 1 inc, 3 sc, 1 inc, 5 sc, 1 inc, 3 sc, 1 inc (34)

R6: 4 sc, 1 inc, 6 sc, 1 inc, 4 sc, 1 inc, 4 sc, 1 inc, 6 sc, 1 inc, 4 sc, 1 inc (40)

R7–9: 1 sc in each st (40)

R10: Working in FLO, 1 sc in each st (40)

Slst in next st. Fasten off, and then weave in the ends with a tapestry needle.

Place the eyes between R7 and R8, about 6 sc apart. Using black yarn, embroider the mouth onto the front of the face with the tapestry needle, just below the eyes.

BELLY

Join the yarn to the first back loop from R10 of the body.

In the next round, we will attach the legs and claws by working through the body and each piece simultaneously. Make sure the claws are oriented as shown and the legs bend downward when attaching.

R1: Working through a leg and the body, sc 3. Working though a claw and the body, sc 3. 6 sc, then, working though the second claw and the body, sc 3. Working though the second leg and the body, sc 3. Working through the third leg and the body, sc 3. Working through the fourth leg and the body, sc 3. 10 sc, then, working though the fifth leg and the body, sc 3. Working through the last leg and the body, sc 3 (40)

R2: 4 sc, 1 dec, 6 sc, 1 dec, 4 sc, 1 dec, 4 sc, 1 dec, 6 sc, 1 dec, 4 sc, 1 dec (34)

R3: 3 sc, 1 dec, 5 sc, 1 dec, 3 sc, 1 dec, 3 sc, 1 dec, 5 sc, 1 dec, 3 sc, 1 dec (28)

R4: 2 sc, 1 dec, 4 sc, 1 dec, 2 sc, 1 dec, 2 sc, 1 dec, 4 sc, 1 dec, 2 sc, 1 dec (22)

R5: 1 sc, 1 dec, 3 sc, 1 dec, 1 sc, 1 dec, 1 sc, 1 dec, 3 sc, 1 dec, 1 sc, 1 dec (16)

R6: 1 dec, 2 sc, 3 dec, 2 sc, 2 dec (10)

Stuff the piece with polyester fiberfill. Stitch along the opening to close off, and then weave in the ends with a tapestry needle.

Body, round 1

Body, placing eyes

Belly, joining yarn

Belly, round 1

Claudia the Crab, finished

ONCE UPON A TIME

Once upon a time, in a land far, far away, there was a beautiful princess. She spent all of her time in the castle and soon grew tired of her day-to-day routine. She longed to let her creativity and imagination run free! One day, a lovely fairy appeared and gave the princess a bit of string and a magic hook. At first, the princess was confused by the gifts. But she soon realized that they could be used to create anything she dreamed of—from silly gnomes (page 55) to friendly ghosts (page 49) and beautiful mermaids (page 51)! Her creations brought joy to all who entered the kingdom.

Unfortunately, most of us don't get to live in a storybook. But, with a bit of practice, patience and hard work, you can still create a little magic of your own!

This chapter is filled with my most mystical, magical and sometimes quirky designs. They are full of personality and will have you dreaming of adventure, magic spells and happily ever afters! So, pick up your crochet hook and settle in, because this is where the magic happens! No matter how old you are, these patterns will remind you of all the delight and wonder from your favorite childhood fairy tales. They will make you believe that anything is possible!

PIPPA
the Princess

Pippa the Princess is beautiful, kind and fair. She is the perfect fairy-tale princess. But she is by no means a damsel in distress! Take a seat, Prince Charming—this girl is smart, sassy and dreams of adventure! Pippa the Princess is worked in continuous rounds and joins together with no sewing necessary. The arms are made first and worked into the body. Then strips of yarn are added to the piece to create the hair and the tassel for her hat. This pattern calls for blonde hair and a light pink dress, but feel free to personalize your princess by picking your favorite colors! Pippa stands about 8 inches (20.5 cm) tall and 3 inches (8 cm) wide.

ARMS

This piece starts at the tip of each arm using tan yarn. Repeat the pattern so you have two arms.

R1: 6 sc in MR (6)

R2–3: 1 sc in each st (6)

Switch to pink yarn.

R4: Working in FLO, 1 inc in each st (12)

R5: 1 sc in each st (12)

R6: 6 dec (6)

Flatten the piece.

R7: Ch 1, turn, then working through the front and back stitches, sc 3

Ch 1 then fasten off. No need to weave in the ends, the yarn will end up inside the piece.

Arms, round 7

(CONTINUED)

MATERIALS

0.5 oz tan worsted weight/4-ply yarn

1.5 oz pink worsted weight/4-ply yarn

0.5 oz yellow worsted weight/4-ply yarn

Size E-4 (3.5 mm) crochet hook

Stitch markers

2 (6-mm) black plastic safety eyes

Scrap pieces of white yarn for details

Polyester fiberfill

Tapestry needle

TERMINOLOGY

R1:	row 1 or round 1
st(s):	stitch(es)
slst:	slip stitch
ch:	chain
sc:	single crochet
inc:	single crochet increase
dec:	invisible decrease
MR:	magic ring
FLO:	front loops only
BLO:	back loops only

Pippa the Princess (Continued)

HAT

This piece starts at the top of the hat using pink yarn.

R1: 6 sc in MR (6)

R2: 1 sc in each st (6)

R3: [1 sc, 1 inc] x3 (9)

R4: 1 sc in each st (9)

R5: [2 sc, 1 inc] x3 (12)

R6: 1 sc in each st (12)

R7: [3 sc, 1 inc] x3 (15)

R8: 1 sc in each st (15)

R9: [4 sc, 1 inc] x3 (18)

R10: 1 sc in each st (18)

R11: [5 sc, 1 inc] x3 (21)

R12: 1 sc in each st (21)

R13: [6 sc, 1 inc] x3 (24)

R14: 1 sc in each st (24)

R15: [7 sc, 1 inc] x3 (27)

R16: 1 sc in each st (27)

R17: [8 sc, 1 inc] x3 (30)

R18: Working in FLO, 1 sc in each st (30)

Slst in next st. Fasten off, and then weave in the ends with a tapestry needle.

HEAD AND BODY

Using tan yarn, join the yarn to the first back loop from R18 of the hat.

R1–4: 1 sc in each st (30)

R5: [3 sc, 1 dec] x6 (24)

R6: [2 sc, 1 dec] x6 (18)

Stuff the piece with polyester fiberfill.

Switch to pink yarn. In the next round, we will attach the arms by working through the body and each arm simultaneously.

R7: 3 sc, then, working through an arm and the body, sc 3. 6 sc. then, working through the second arm and the body, sc 3. 3 sc (18)

Place the eyes between R3 and R4, about 6 sc apart.

R8–10: 1 sc in each st (18)

R11: Working in FLO, [2 sc, 1 inc] x6 (24)

R12: [3 sc, 1 inc] x6 (30)

R13: [4 sc, 1 inc] x6 (36)

R14–21: 1 sc in each st (36)

R22: Working in BLO, [4 sc, 1 dec] x6 (30)

R23: [3 sc, 1 dec] x6 (24)

R24: [2 sc, 1 dec] x6 (18)

R25: [1 sc, 1 dec] x6 (12)

R26: 6 dec (6)

Stuff the piece with polyester fiberfill. Close off, and then weave in the ends with a tapestry needle.

BELT

Use white yarn for this piece.

Ch 18 (18)

Finish off. Use the yarn ends to attach the belt to your princess's waist and tie a bow.

(CONTINUED)

Hat and head, joining yarn

Head and body, round 7

Head and body, finished

Belt, finished

Pippa the Princess (Continued)

FINISHING

Hair: Cut at least 30 pieces of yellow yarn approximately 12 inches (30 cm) in length. Fold each piece of yarn in half and draw up a loop through a stitch in the head. Pull the yarn ends through the loop and tighten. Repeat as needed to cover the head. Note: The strands of hair can be spaced out to reduce bulk. Gaps will not be visible when the hair is down. Trim the hair as needed.

Tassel: Cut 2 pieces of pink yarn and 2 pieces of white yarn, each approximately 12 inches (30 cm) in length. Holding all 4 strands together, fold the yarn in half and draw up a loop through the top of the hat. Pull the yarn ends through the loop and tighten.

Finishing, hair

Finishing, tassel

Nessie
the Loch Ness Monster

Through thick fog and frigid waters, something mysterious lurks in the distance. Her long neck and humped back slowly emerge from the surface of the lake. But luckily, this mystical creature is as friendly as can be. Her cute and cuddly stature makes her the perfect companion! Nessie the Loch Ness Monster is worked in continuous rounds and joins together seamlessly with no sewing necessary. The techniques used in this pattern are more advanced and call for joining separate pieces and working in free loops to give Nessie her unique shape. This pattern uses light green yarn, but feel free to personalize your Nessie by picking your favorite colors! Nessie swims about 6 inches (15.5 cm) tall and 7 inches (18 cm) long.

FINS

This piece starts at the tip of each fin. Repeat the pattern until you have four fins.

R1: 4 sc in MR (4)

R2: [1 sc, 1 inc] x2 (6)

R3: [1 sc, 1 inc] x3 (9)

R4: [2 sc, 1 inc] x3 (12)

R5: 1 sc in each st (12)

R6: 6 dec (6)

Flatten the piece.

R7: Ch 1, turn, then working through the front and back stitches, sc 3 (3)

Slst in next st and fasten off. No need to weave in the ends, the yarn will end up inside the piece.

Fins, round 7

(CONTINUED)

MATERIALS

1.5 oz light green worsted weight/4-ply yarn

Size E-4 (3.5 mm) crochet hook

Stitch markers

2 (6-mm) black plastic safety eyes

Polyester fiberfill

Tapestry needle

TERMINOLOGY

R1:	row 1 or round 1
st(s):	stitch(es)
slst:	slip stitch
ch:	chain
sc:	single crochet
inc:	single crochet increase
dec:	invisible decrease
MR:	magic ring

Nessie the Loch Ness Monster (Continued)

HUMP

This piece starts at the top of the hump using a foundation chain to create an oval.

R1: Ch 7 to create a foundation chain. Starting at the second chain from the hook, sc 5 in the back loops of the foundation chain. 1 inc in the last stitch, rotate the chain, then 1 sc in the front loop of the same stitch. sc 4 in the front loops, then inc in the last stitch (14)

R2: 1 inc, 4 sc, 1 inc, 1 sc, 1 inc, 4 sc, 2 inc (19)

R3: 1 sc, 1 inc, 5 sc, 1 inc, 2 sc, 1 inc, 5 sc, 1 inc, 1 sc, 1 inc (24)

R4: 1 sc, 1 inc, 6 sc, 1 inc, 3 sc, 1 inc, 6 sc, 1 inc, 2 sc, 1 inc, 1 sc (29)

Fasten off. No need to weave in the ends, the yarn will end up inside the piece.

Hump, round 1

HEAD

This piece starts at the top of the head.

R1: 6 sc in MR (6)

R2: 1 inc in each st (12)

R3: [1 sc, 1 inc] x6 (18)

R4: [2 sc, 1 inc] x6 (24)

R5: 8 sc, then place a stitch marker on st 8 to mark a space for the eyes. 8 sc, then place a stitch marker on st 16. 8 sc (24)

R6–7: 1 sc in each st (24)

Place the eyes between R5 and R6 where you placed your stitch markers.

R8: 6 sc, 6 dec, 6 sc (18)

R9: 3 sc, 6 dec, 3 sc (12)

Stuff the head with polyester fiberfill.

R10–19: 1 sc in each st (12)

After R19, work 2 sc so the yarn end lines up with the back of the neck. Stuff the neck with polyester fiberfill. Leave your hook in the last stitch and proceed to the body.

Head, finished

(CONTINUED)

Nessie the Loch Ness Monster (Continued)

BODY

Hold the head and hump together as shown. The eyes should be facing forward, and the yarn end of the hump should be facing backwards. With the last loop of the neck still on your hook, slst 1 through both pieces to join. To begin the next round, start by crocheting clockwise around both pieces, excluding the slst used to join the pieces.

R1: 1 sc in each st (38)

R2: 21 sc, 1 inc, 5 sc, 1 inc, 10 sc (40)

R3: 22 sc, 1 inc, 6 sc, 1 inc, 10 sc (42)

R4: 24 sc, ch 6, skip 6 sts to create the hole for the tail, 12 sc (42)

R5: 1 sc in each st (42)

In the next round, we will attach the fins by working through the body and each fin simultaneously.

R6: 11 sc, then, working through a fin and the body, sc 3. 5 sc, then, working through the second fin and the body, sc 3. 9 sc, then, working through the third fin and the body, sc 3. 5 sc, then, working through the last fin and the body sc 3 (42)

R7: 1 dec, 3 sc, 1 dec, 3 sc, 1 dec, 9 sc, 1 dec, 3 sc, 1 dec, 3 sc, 1 dec, 9 sc (36)

R8: 1 dec, 2 sc, 1 dec, 2 sc, 1 dec, 8 sc, 1 dec, 2 sc, 1 dec, 2 sc, 1 dec, 8 sc (30)

R9: 1 dec, 1 sc, 1 dec, 1 sc, 1 dec, 7 sc, 1 dec, 1 sc, 1 dec, 1 sc, 1 dec, 7 sc (24)

R10: 3 dec, 6 sc, 3 dec, 6 sc (18)

R11: 2 dec, 5 sc, 2 dec, 5 sc (14)

Stuff the body with polyester fiberfill. Stitch along the opening to close off, and then weave in the ends with a tapestry needle.

TAIL

Going clockwise, rejoin the yarn at the leg of the sc adjacent to the end of the tail chain as shown.

R1: Using the leg of the adjacent sc and the first stitch of the body, 1 dec. 5 sc (of the body), 6 sc (of the tail chain) (12)

R2: 2 sc, 1 dec, 8 sc (11)

R3: 2 sc, 1 dec, 7 sc (10)

R4: 2 sc, 1 dec, 6 sc (9)

R5: 2 sc, 1 dec, 5 sc (8)

Stuff the tail with polyester fiberfill.

R6: 2 sc, 1 dec, 4 sc (7)

R7: 2 sc, 1 dec, 3 sc (6)

R8: 2 sc, 1 dec, 2 sc (5)

R9: 2 sc, 1 dec, 1 sc (4)

Close off, and then weave in the ends with a tapestry needle.

Body, joining

Body, round 4

Body, round 6

Body, finished

Tail, round 1

Nessie the Loch Ness Monster, finished

AMOR
the Love Potion

If you have a secret crush and are dying to tell them how you feel, Amor the Love Potion might just do the trick. No magic, bat wings or toadstool necessary. Amor's adorable blushing face will win them over in a heartbeat! Amor the Love Potion is worked in continuous rounds and joins together with no sewing necessary. This pattern calls for red yarn, but try pink yarn if you want a softer look. Or change up the colors and make any potion you like—dragon's breath, snake venom or elixir of life! Amor stands at approximately 4.5 inches (11.5 cm) tall and 3 inches (8 cm) wide.

BOTTLE

This piece starts at the bottom of the bottle using red yarn.

R1: 6 sc in MR (6)

R2: 1 inc in each st (12)

R3: [1 sc, 1 inc] x6 (18)

R4: [2 sc, 1 inc] x6 (24)

R5: Working in BLO, [3 sc, 1 inc] x6 (30)

R6–11: 1 sc in each st (30)

Place the eyes between R8 and R9, about 4 sc apart. Using black yarn, embroider the mouth onto the front of the face with the tapestry needle, just below the eyes.

R12: [3 sc, 1 dec] x6 (24)

R13: [2 sc, 1 dec] x6 (18)

R14: [1 sc, 1 dec] x6 (12)

Stuff the piece with polyester fiberfill.

R15–16: 1 sc in each st (12)

Change to white yarn.

R17–20: 1 sc in each st (12)

R21: Working in FLO, 1 sc in each st (12)

Fasten off, and then weave in the ends with a tapestry needle.

CORK

Using tan yarn, join the yarn to the first back loop from R21 of the bottle.

R1–3: 1 sc in each st (12)

R4: Working in BLO, 6 sc2tog (6)

Stuff the piece with polyester fiberfill. Close off, and then weave in the ends with a tapestry needle.

Cork, joining yarn

Bottle, finished

MATERIALS

0.5 oz red worsted weight/4-ply yarn

0.5 oz white worsted weight/4-ply yarn

0.5 oz tan worsted weight/4-ply yarn

Size E-4 (3.5 mm) crochet hook

Stitch markers

2 (6-mm) black plastic safety eyes

Scrap piece of black yarn for embroidery

Polyester fiberfill

Tapestry needle

TERMINOLOGY

R1:	row 1 or round 1
st(s):	stitch(es)
sc:	single crochet
inc:	single crochet increase
dec:	invisible decrease
sc2tog:	single crochet two together
MR:	magic ring
FLO:	front loops only
BLO:	back loops only

Boo
the Ghost

Ghosts don't exactly have the best reputation. They are notorious for howling in the wind, flickering your lights and sending a chill down your spine. But not Boo the Ghost. He just wants to tell you that he thinks you're boo-tiful, fa-boo-lous and drop-dead gorgeous! Boo the Ghost is worked in continuous rounds and joins together with no sewing necessary. The arms are made first and worked into the body. Add a string to the top of Boo's head and hang him up high so he can levitate! Boo floats about 5 inches (3 cm) tall and 3 inches (8 cm) wide.

MATERIALS

1 oz white worsted weight/4-ply yarn

Size E-4 (3.5 mm) crochet hook

Stitch markers

2 (6-mm) black plastic safety eyes

Polyester fiberfill

Tapestry needle

TERMINOLOGY

R1:	row 1 or round 1
st(s):	stitch(es)
ch:	chain
sc:	single crochet
inc:	single crochet increase
dec:	invisible decrease
MR:	magic ring

ARMS

This piece starts at the tip of each arm. Repeat the pattern so you have two arms.

R1: 6 sc in MR (6)

R2–4: 1 sc in each st (6)

Flatten the piece.

R5: Ch 1, turn, then working through the front and back stitches, sc 3 (3)

Ch 1 then fasten off. No need to weave in the ends, the yarn will end up inside the piece.

HEAD AND BODY

This piece starts at the top of the head.

R1: 6 sc in MR (6)

R2: 1 inc in each st (12)

R3: [1 sc, 1 inc] x6 (18)

R4: [2 sc, 1 inc] x6 (24)

R5: [3 sc, 1 inc] x6 (30)

R6–11: 1 sc in each st (36)

R12: [3 sc, 1 dec] x6 (24)

R13: [2 sc, 1 dec] x6 (18)

In the next round, we will attach the arms by working through the body and each arm simultaneously.

R14: 3 sc, then, working through an arm and the body, sc 3. 6 sc, then, working through the second arm and the body, sc 3. 3 sc (18)

Place the eyes between R9 and R10, about 6 sc apart. Stuff the piece with polyester fiberfill.

R15: [5 sc, 1 inc] x3 (21)

R16: [6 sc, 1 inc] x3 (24)

R17–19: 1 sc in each st (24)

R20: [2 sc, 1 dec] x6 (18)

R21: 4 sc, 1 dec, [1 sc, 1 dec] x3, 3 sc (14)

R22: 3 sc, 4 dec, 3 sc (10)

R23: 1 sc, 4 dec, 1 sc (6)

Stuff the piece with polyester fiberfill. Close off, and then weave in the ends with a tapestry needle.

Arms, round 5

Head and body, round 14

CORAL
the Mermaid

Snorkeling in beautiful, crystal clear waters is one of my favorite vacation activities. I get to explore the depths of the ocean, swim alongside turtles and unleash my inner mermaid. Now, if only I could have their fabulous hair and seashells. Coral the Mermaid is worked in continuous rounds and joins together with no sewing necessary. Starting with the arms allows them to be worked into the body. Then each side of the tail is made separately and joined together to create a seamless piece. To finish, an itsy-bitsy bikini is attached to her torso and then strips of yarn are added to her head to create long flowing hair. This pattern calls for brown hair and a light purple bikini, but feel free to personalize your mermaid by picking your favorite colors! Coral swims at about 7 inches (18 cm) tall and 3 inches (8 cm) wide.

MATERIALS

0.5 oz tan worsted weight/4-ply yarn

0.5 oz light green worsted weight/4-ply yarn

0.5 oz light purple worsted weight/4-ply yarn

0.5 oz dark brown worsted weight/4-ply yarn

Size E-4 (3.5 mm) crochet hook

Stitch markers

2 (6-mm) black plastic safety eyes

Polyester fiberfill

Tapestry needle

ARMS

This piece starts at the tip of each arm using tan yarn. Repeat the pattern so that you have two arms.

R1: 6 sc in MR (6)

R2-4: 1 sc in each st (6)

Flatten the piece.

R5: Ch 1, turn, then, working through the front and back stitches, sc 3 (3)

Ch 1 then fasten off. No need to weave in the ends, the yarn will end up inside the piece.

Arms, finished

(CONTINUED)

TERMINOLOGY

R1:	row 1 or round 1
st(s):	stitch(es)
slst:	slip stitch
ch:	chain
sc:	single crochet
inc:	single crochet increase
dec:	invisible decrease
hdc:	half double crochet
MR:	magic ring
BLO:	back loops only

FIN PART 1

This piece starts at the tip of the fin using light green yarn.

R1: 4 sc in MR (4)

R2: [1 sc, 1 inc] x2 (6)

R3: [1 sc, 1 inc] x3 (9)

R4: [2 sc, 1 inc] x3 (12)

R5: [2 sc, 1 dec] x3 (9)

Slst in next st and fasten off.

Coral the Mermaid (Continued)

FIN PART 2

This piece starts at the tip of the fin using light green yarn.

R1: 4 sc in MR (4)

R2: [1 sc, 1 inc] x2 (6)

R3: [1 sc, 1 inc] x3 (9)

R4: [2 sc, 1 inc] x3 (12)

R5: [2 sc, 1 dec] x3 (9)

TAIL AND BODY

Leave your hook in the last stitch and proceed to the body head. Hold the fin sections together as shown. With the last loop of the fin piece still on your hook, slst 1 through both pieces to join. To begin the next round, start by crocheting clockwise around both pieces, excluding the slst used to join.

R1: 2 sc, 2 dec, 4 sc, 2 dec, 2 sc (12)

R2: 6 dec (6)

R3: [1 sc, 1 inc] x3 (9)

R4: [2 sc, 1 inc] x3 (12)

R5: [3 sc, 1 inc] x3 (15)

R6: 1 sc in each st (15)

R7: [4 sc, 1 inc] x3 (18)

R8: 1 sc in each st (18)

R9: [5 sc, 1 inc] x3 (21)

R10: 1 sc in each st (21)

R11: [6 sc, 1 inc] x3 (24)

R12: 1 sc in each st (24)

R13: 1 sc in each st (24)

R14: [2 sc, 1 dec] x6 (18)

Switch to tan yarn.

R15: Working in BLO, 1 sc in each st (18)

R16: 1 sc in each st (18)

R17: 1 sc in each st (18)

In the next round, we will attach the arms by working through the body and each arm simultaneously.

R18: 6 sc, then, working through an arm and the body, sc 3. 6 sc, then, working through the second arm and the body, sc 3 (18)

Stuff the piece with polyester fiberfill.

R19: [2 sc, 1 inc] x6 (24)

R20: [3 sc, 1 inc] x6 (30)

R21-26: 1 sc in each st (30)

Place the eyes between R21 and R22, about 6 sc apart.

R27: [3 sc, 1 dec] x6 (24)

R28: [2 sc, 1 dec] x6 (18)

R29: [1 sc, 1 dec] x6 (12)

R30: 6 dec (6)

Stuff the piece with polyester fiberfill. Close off, and then weave in the ends with a tapestry needle.

WAIST DETAIL

Using light green yarn, join the yarn to the center front loop of R15 of the body.

R1: 1 slst, 1 sc, 15 hdc, 1 sc (18)

Slst in next st and fasten off.

(CONTINUED)

Fin part 1 and 2, joining

Tail and body, round 1

Tail and body, round 18

Waist detail, joining yarn

Coral the Mermaid (Continued)

BIKINI

Use light purple yarn for this piece.

Ch 19 to create a foundation chain. Starting at the second chain from hook, sc 18 (18)

Use the yarn ends to tie the top onto the body and weave in the ends with a tapestry needle. Feel free to try out different bikini styles!

FINISHING

Cut at least 50 pieces of dark brown yarn, each approximately 12 inches (30 cm) in length. Fold each piece of yarn in half and draw up a loop through a stitch in the head. Pull the yarn ends through the loop and tighten.

Repeat as needed to cover the head. The strands of hair can be spaced out to reduce bulk. Gaps will not be visible when the hair is down. Trim the hair as needed. I like to part the hair and tie a little knot on the side of the head to hold it into place.

Finishing

Coral the Mermaid, finished

NORM
the Gnome

I'm not sure when or why it became popular to place a statue of a short-bearded man in your garden. But there is no denying that these silly little creatures radiate personality, warmth and humor. Make your own Norm to add a little fun and whimsy to your life! Norm the Gnome is worked in continuous rounds and joins together with no sewing necessary. For this pattern, he sports a classic red hat and green shirt, but feel free to switch it up! The techniques used in this pattern are more advanced. We'll create each leg and join them together to create a seamless piece. Then we'll leave a few sections of free loops to add his beard, the brim of his hat and the bottom of his shirt. Norm stands at a modest 6 inches (15.5 cm) tall and 3 inches (8 cm) wide.

MATERIALS

0.5 oz tan worsted weight/4-ply yarn

0.5 oz light green worsted weight/4-ply yarn

0.5 oz dark brown worsted weight/4-ply yarn

0.5 oz light blue worsted weight/ 4-ply yarn

0.5 oz white worsted weight/4-ply yarn

0.5 oz red worsted weight/4-ply yarn

Size E-4 (3.5 mm) crochet hook

Stitch markers

2 (6-mm) black plastic safety eyes

Polyester fiberfill

Tapestry needle

ARMS

This piece starts at the tip of each arm using tan yarn. Repeat this pattern so you have two arms.

R1: 6 sc in MR (6)

R2: 1 sc in each st (6)

Switch to light green yarn.

R3–4: 1 sc in each st (6)

Flatten the piece.

R5: Ch 1, turn, then, working through the front and back stitches, sc 3 (3)

Ch 1 then fasten off. No need to weave in the ends, the yarn will end up inside the piece.

Arms, finished

NOSE

This piece starts at the tip of the nose using tan yarn.

R1: 6 sc in MR (6)

Fold the piece in half.

R2: Ch 1, turn, then working through the front and back stitches, sc 3 (3)

Ch 1 then fasten off. No need to weave in the ends, the yarn will end up inside the piece.

Nose, finished

(CONTINUED)

TERMINOLOGY

R1:	row 1 or round 1
st(s):	stitch(es)
slst:	slip stitch
ch:	chain
sc:	single crochet
inc:	single crochet increase
dec:	invisible decrease
sc2tog:	single crochet two together
MR:	magic ring
BLO:	back loops only

Norm the Gnome (Continued)

RIGHT LEG

This piece starts at the bottom of the foot using dark brown yarn.

R1: 6 sc in MR (6)

R2: 1 inc in each st (12)

R3: Working in BLO, 1 sc in each st (12)

R4: 5 sc, 3 dec, 1 sc (9)

Switch to light blue yarn.

R5: 1 sc in each st (9)

Slst in next st and fasten off.

LEFT LEG

This piece starts at the bottom of the foot using dark brown yarn.

R1: 6 sc in MR (6)

R2: 1 inc in each st (12)

R3: Working in BLO, 1 sc in each st (12)

R4: 5 sc, 3 dec, 1 sc (9)

Switch to light blue yarn.

R5: 1 sc in each st (9)

Leave your hook in the last stitch and proceed to the body.

BODY AND HEAD

Hold the leg sections together as shown with the feet facing forward. With the last loop of the leg piece still on your hook, slst 1 through both pieces to join.

To begin the next round, start by crocheting clockwise around both pieces, excluding the slst used to join the pieces.

R1: 1 sc in each st (16)

R2: 2 sc, 1 inc, 10 sc, 1 inc, 2 sc (18)

R3: 1 sc in each st (18)

Switch to dark brown yarn.

R4: Working in BLO, 1 sc in each st (18)

Switch to green yarn.

R5: 1 sc in each st (18)

(CONTINUED)

Right leg, finished

Right and left legs, joining

Body and head, round 6

Norm the Gnome (Continued)

R6: 1 sc in each st (18)

In the next round, we will attach the arms by working through the body and each arm simultaneously.

R7: 4 sc, then, working through an arm and body, sc 3. 6 sc, then, working through the second arm and the body, sc 3. 2 sc (18)

Stuff the piece with polyester fiberfill. Switch to white yarn.

R8: [2 sc, 1 inc] x6 (24)

R9: [3 sc, 1 inc] x6 (30)

R10: 1 sc in each st (30)

In the next round, we will attach the nose by working through the body and nose simultaneously.

R11: Continuing in white yarn, 10 sc. Switching to tan yarn and working in BLO, 5 sc. Working through the nose and the BLO of the head, sc 3. Working in BLO, 5 sc. Switching to white yarn, 7 sc (30)

R12: Continuing in white yarn, 10 sc. Switching to tan yarn, 13 sc. Switching to white yarn, 7 sc (30)

R13: Continuing in white yarn, 10 sc. Switching to tan yarn, 13 sc. Switching to white yarn, 7 sc (30)

Place the eyes between R11 and R12, about 7 sc apart. Using white yarn, embroider eyebrows diagonally above each eye with the tapestry needle.

Switch to red yarn.

R14: Working in BLO, [8 sc, 1 sc2tog] x3 (27)

R15: [7 sc, 1 dec] x3 (24)

R16: [6 sc, 1 dec] x3 (21)

R17: [5 sc, 1 dec] x3 (18)

R18: [4 sc, 1 dec] x3 (15)

R19: [3 sc, 1 dec] x3 (12)

R20: [2 sc, 1 dec] x3 (9)

R21: [1 sc, 1 dec] x3 (6)

Stuff the piece with polyester fiberfill. Close off, and then weave in the ends with a tapestry needle.

SHIRT

Using light green yarn, join the yarn to the first front loop from R4 of the body.

R1: 1 sc in each st (18)

R2: 1 sc in each st (18)

Fasten off, and then weave in the ends with a tapestry needle.

BEARD

Using white yarn, join the yarn to the first front loop from R11 of the body. For this piece, we will be working back and forth in rows.

R1: 1 sc in each st (13)

R2: Ch 1, turn, 1 dec, 9 sc, 1 dec (11)

R3: Ch 1, turn, 1 dec, 7 sc, 1 dec (9)

R4: Ch 1, turn, 1 dec, 5 sc, 1 dec (7)

R5: Ch 1, turn, 1 dec, 3 sc, 1 dec (5)

R6: Ch 1, turn, 1 dec, 1 sc, 1 dec (3)

R7: Ch 1, turn, sc 3 together (1)

Fasten off, and then weave in the ends with a tapestry needle.

BRIM

Using red yarn, join the yarn to the first front loop from R14 of the body.

R1: 1 sc in each st (30)

Fasten off, and then weave in the ends with a tapestry needle.

Body and head, round 11

Body and head, placing eyes

Body and head, finished

Shirt, joining yarn

Beard, joining yarn

Brim, joining yarn

EAT YOUR HEART OUT

Some of the biggest (and smallest) moments in life are centered around food. Whether it's sweet, salty, savory or sour, the memories you create with your loved ones as you sit down and enjoy a meal together will last a lifetime. Celebrate those special moments with friends and family by making cute and cuddly versions of all their favorites!

Cinna the Cinnamon Roll (page 89) is the perfect gift for mom to remind her of those cherished moments you shared in the kitchen, covered head to toe in flour and sugar. Or make Ike the Ice Cream Scoop (page 77) for the brother who offered to share his cone with you after you dropped yours on the floor. Walter the Watermelon (page 87) and Patty the Pie (page 63) perfectly encapsulate those summer backyard barbeques with friends, while Xavier the Egg (page 69) and Todd the Toast (page 81) are reminiscent of that quiet moment at the breakfast table before the chaos of the day sets in.

Nothing brings people together better than good food. So, eat your heart out with the oodles of decadently sweet treats and lusciously savory bites this chapter has to offer. I hope you're hungry, because we are just getting started!

PaTTy
the Pie

There's nothing quite like a fresh baked pie with a big dollop of whipped cream cooling on the windowsill at grandma's house. I can almost smell Patty's buttery flaky crust and sweet filling. Patty the Pie is worked in continuous rounds with no sewing necessary. For this pattern, we start with the base of the pie, leaving a round of free loops to attach the pie crust. This pattern calls for red filling, but feel free to personalize your pie! Patty's finished size is approximately 3 inches (8 cm) tall and 4.5 inches (11.5 cm) wide.

MATERIALS

0.5 oz golden-brown worsted weight/4-ply yarn

0.5 oz red worsted weight/4-ply yarn

0.5 oz white worsted weight/4-ply yarn

Size E-4 (3.5 mm) crochet hook

Stitch markers

2 (6-mm) black plastic safety eyes

Scrap piece of black yarn for embroidery

Polyester fiberfill

Tapestry needle

Cosmetic blush, for adding cheeks (optional)

PIE

This piece starts at the bottom of the pie using golden-brown yarn.

R1: 6 sc in MR (6)

R2: 1 inc in each st (12)

R3: [1 sc, 1 inc] x6 (18)

R4: [2 sc, 1 inc] x6 (24)

R5: [3 sc, 1 inc] x6 (30)

R6: [4 sc, 1 inc] x6 (36)

R7: [5 sc, 1 inc] x6 (42)

R8: Working in BLO, 1 sc in each st (42)

R9: [13 sc, 1 inc] x3 (45)

R10: 1 sc in each st (45)

R11: [14 sc, 1 inc] x3 (48)

Switch to red yarn.

R12: Working in BLO, [6 sc, 1 sc2tog] x6 (42)

R13: [5 sc, 1 dec] x6 (36)

R14: [4 sc, 1 dec] x6 (30)

R15: [3 sc, 1 dec] x6 (24)

R16: [2 sc, 1 dec] x6 (18)

R17: [1 sc, 1 dec] x6 (12)

Place the eyes between R14 and R15, about 4 sc apart. Using black yarn, embroider the mouth onto the front of the face with the tapestry needle, just below the eyes. Add blush for rosy pink cheeks, if you'd like. Stuff the piece with polyester fiberfill.

Switch to white yarn.

R18: [1 sc, 1 inc] x6 (18)

R19: 1 sc in each st (18)

R20: [1 sc, 1 dec] x6 (12)

R21: 6 dec (6)

R22: 3 dec (3)

Stuff the piece with polyester fiberfill. Close off, and then weave in the ends with a tapestry needle.

PIE CRUST

Using golden-brown yarn, join the yarn to the first front loop from R12 of the pie.

R1: [1 slst, 3 hdc in the next st] x21 (84)

Slst in next st. Fasten off, and then weave in the ends with a tapestry needle.

Pie crust, round 1

TERMINOLOGY

R1:	row 1 or round 1
st(s):	stitch(es)
slst:	slip stitch
sc:	single crochet
inc:	single crochet increase
dec:	invisible decrease
sc2tog:	single crochet two together
hdc:	half double crochet
MR:	magic ring
BLO:	back loops only

PHOEBE AND JAY

the PB & J

In a list of perfect pairs—milk and cookies, ketchup and mustard, Ross and Rachel—one of my favorites has to be peanut butter and jelly. The deliciously sweet and salty combination is a classic! Crochet your own and I guarantee Phoebe and Jay will have you craving PB & J's all day long! Phoebe and Jay are worked in continuous rounds and join together seamlessly with no sewing necessary. They each follow the same pattern, all you need to do is switch out the colors. Use brown yarn for Phoebe and light purple yarn for Jay. Phoebe and Jay's finished sizes are approximately 4 inches (10 cm) tall and 3 inches (8 cm) wide.

JAR

This piece starts at the bottom of the jar using golden-brown (or light purple) yarn.

R1: 6 sc in MR (6)

R2: 1 inc in each st (12)

R3: [1 sc, 1 inc] x6 (18)

R4: [2 sc, 1 inc] x6 (24)

R5: [3 sc, 1 inc] x6 (30)

R6: [4 sc, 1 inc] x6 (36)

R7: Working in BLO, 1 sc in each st (36)

R8–10: 1 sc in each st (36)

Switch to white yarn.

R11–16: 1 sc in each st (36)

Place the eyes between R12 and R13, about 4 sc apart. Using black yarn, embroider the mouth onto the front of the face with the tapestry needle, just below the eyes. Add blush for rosy pink cheeks, if you'd like.

Switch to golden-brown (or light purple) yarn.

R17–20: 1 sc in each st (36)

R21: [4 sc, 1 dec] x6 (30)

R22: 1 sc in each st (30)

Switch to red (or purple) yarn.

R23–24: 1 sc each st (30)

R25: Working in BLO, [3 sc, 1 sc2tog] x6 (24)

R26: [2 sc, 1 dec] x6 (18)

R27: [1 sc, 1 dec] x6 (12)

R28: 6 dec (6)

Stuff the piece with polyester fiberfill. Close off, and then weave in the ends with a tapestry needle.

SKILL LEVEL

MATERIALS

1 oz golden-brown worsted weight/4-ply yarn

0.5 oz white worsted weight/4-ply yarn

0.5 oz red worsted weight/4-ply yarn

1 oz light purple worsted weight/4-ply yarn (optional)

0.5 oz purple worsted weight/4-ply yarn (optional)

Size E-4 (3.5 mm) crochet hook

Stitch markers

2 (6-mm) black plastic safety eyes

Scrap piece of black yarn for embroidery

Polyester fiberfill

Tapestry needle

Cosmetic blush, for cheeks (optional)

TERMINOLOGY

R1:	row 1 or round 1
st(s):	stitch(es)
sc:	single crochet
inc:	single crochet increase
dec:	invisible decrease
sc2tog:	single crochet two together
MR:	magic ring
BLO:	back loops only

COCO
the Coconut

During our trip to Maui, my fiancé and I would spend hours lounging on the beach surrounded by sun and coconuts. On our last day, he was determined to crack one open, just to see if he could survive on a deserted island. This man drives me coconuts, but I love him to pieces! Coco the Coconut is worked in continuous rounds and joins together seamlessly with no sewing necessary. The white part of the coconut is inverted into the brown part to create its concave shape. Coco's finished size is approximately 4 inches (10 cm) tall and 2 inches (5 cm) wide.

SKILL LEVEL

MATERIALS

1 oz white worsted weight/4-ply yarn

1 oz dark brown worsted weight/ 4-ply yarn

Size E-4 (3.5 mm) crochet hook

Stitch markers

Scrap piece of black yarn for embroidery

Tapestry needle

Cosmetic blush, for adding cheeks (optional)

COCONUT

This piece starts at the center of the coconut using white yarn.

R1: 6 sc in MR (6)

R2: 1 inc in each st (12)

R3: [1 sc, 1 inc] x6 (18)

R4: [2 sc, 1 inc] x6 (24)

R5: [3 sc, 1 inc] x6 (30)

R6: [4 sc, 1 inc] x6 (36)

R7: [5 sc, 1 inc] x6 (42)

R8: [6 sc, 1 inc] x6 (48)

R9–13: 1 sc in each st (48)

Using black yarn, embroider the eyes and mouth onto the inside of the coconut at the center of the piece. Add blush for rosy pink cheeks, if you'd like.

R14: Working in BLO, [7 sc, 1 inc] x6 (54)

Change to brown yarn.

R15: Working in BLO, 1 sc in each st (54)

R16–20: 1 sc in each st (54)

R21: [7 sc, 1 dec] x6 (48)

R22: [6 sc, 1 dec] x6 (42)

R23: [5 sc, 1 dec] x6 (36)

R24: [4 sc, 1 dec] x6 (30)

R25: [3 sc, 1 dec] x6 (24)

R26: [2 sc, 1 dec] x6 (18)

R27: [1 sc, 1 dec] x6 (12)

R28: 6 dec (6)

No stuffing necessary. Close off, and then weave in the ends with a tapestry needle.

TERMINOLOGY

R1:	row 1 or round 1
st(s):	stitch(es)
sc:	single crochet
inc:	single crochet increase
dec:	invisible decrease
MR:	magic ring
BLO:	back loops only

Coco the Coconut, finished

XAVIER
the Egg

Xavier the egg was inspired by that moment when you cut into a perfectly cooked egg and the oozy yolk spills out onto your plate. It is truly a thing of beauty and instantly makes any meal more decadent and delicious. So, I hope you're eggcited to make one of your own! Xavier the Egg is worked in continuous rounds and joins together with no sewing necessary. The pattern starts with the egg yolk, leaving a round of free loops to attach the egg white. Then we use a few half double crochets around the border to give Xavier shape. Xavier's finished size is approximately 1 inch (2.5 cm) tall and 4 inches (10 cm) wide.

MATERIALS

0.5 oz yellow worsted weight/4-ply yarn

0.5 oz white worsted weight/4-ply yarn

Size E-4 (3.5 mm) crochet hook

Stitch markers

2 (6-mm) black plastic safety eyes

Scrap piece of black yarn for embroidery

Polyester fiberfill

Tapestry needle

Cosmetic blush, for adding cheeks (optional)

TERMINOLOGY

R1:	row 1 or round 1
st(s):	stitch(es)
slst:	slip stitch
sc:	single crochet
inc:	single crochet increase
dec:	invisible decrease
hdc:	half double crochet
sc2tog:	single crochet two together
MR:	magic ring
BLO:	back loops only

YOLK

This piece starts at the center of the yolk using yellow yarn.

R1: 6 sc in MR (6)

R2: 1 inc in each st (12)

R3: [1 sc, 1 inc] x6 (18)

R4: [2 sc, 1 inc] x6 (24)

R5-6: 1 sc in each st (24)

Place the eyes between R3 and R4, about 6 st apart. Using black yarn, embroider the mouth onto the front of the face with the tapestry needle, just below the eyes. Add blush for rosy pink cheeks, if you'd like.

R7: Working in BLO, [2 sc, 1 sc2tog] x6 (18)

R8: [1 sc, 1 dec] x6 (12)

R9: 6 dec (6)

Stuff the piece with polyester fiberfill. Close off, and weave in the ends with a tapestry needle.

EGG WHITE

Using white yarn, join the yarn to the first front loop from R7 of the yolk.

R1: [3 sc, 1 inc] x6 (30)

R2: [4 sc, 1 inc] x6 (36)

R3: [5 sc, 1 inc] x6 (42)

R4: [6 sc, 1 inc] x6 (48)

R5: 4 sc, 3 hdc, 2 hdc in next st, 2 hdc, 3 sc, 2 hdc, 2 hdc in next st, 6 sc, 1 hdc, 2 hdc in next st, 4 hdc, 3 sc, 1 inc, 5 sc, 2 hdc, 2 hdc in next st, 3 hdc, 4 sc, 1 inc (54)

Slst in next st. Fasten off, and then weave in the ends with a tapestry needle.

Yolk, finished

Egg white, joining yarn

GRAHAM
the S'more

When I'm not buried under a pile of yarn, I like to disconnect from the world, hike through rugged terrain and marvel at breathtaking landscapes. At the end of the night, my friends and I roast marshmallows and share stories around a roaring fire. It's the perfect ending to a day filled with wonder and adventure. Graham the S'more is composed of four separate pieces that stack together. The marshmallow is worked in continuous rounds, but the graham crackers and chocolate are worked in rows. Then we add a border to the graham crackers and chocolate to create a clean and polished look. Graham's finished size is approximately 2.5 x 2.5 x 2.5 inches (6.5 x 6.5 x 6.5 cm).

MARSHMALLOW

This piece starts at the top of the marshmallow using white yarn.

R1: 6 sc in MR (6)

R2: 1 inc in each st (12)

R3: [1 sc, 1 inc] x6 (18)

R4: [2 sc, 1 inc] x6 (24)

R5: Working in BLO, 1 sc in each st (24)

R6–12: 1 sc in each st (24)

Place the eyes between R8 and R9, about 4 sc apart. Using black yarn, embroider the mouth onto the front of the face with the tapestry needle, just below the eyes. Add blush for rosy pink cheeks, if you'd like.

R13: Working in BLO, [2 sc, 1 sc2tog] x6 (18)

R14: [1 sc, 1 dec] x6 (12)

R15: 6 dec (6)

Stuff the piece with polyester fiberfill. Close off, and then weave in the ends with a tapestry needle.

Marshmallow, finished

(CONTINUED)

MATERIALS

0.5 oz white worsted weight/4-ply yarn

0.5 oz golden-brown worsted weight/4-ply yarn

0.5 oz dark brown worsted weight/4-ply yarn

Size E-4 (3.5 mm) crochet hook

2 (6-mm) black plastic safety eyes

Scrap piece of black yarn for embroidery

Polyester fiberfill

Tapestry needle

Cosmetic blush, for adding cheeks (optional)

TERMINOLOGY

R1:	row 1 or round 1
st(s):	stitch(es)
slst:	slip stitch
ch:	chain
sc:	single crochet
inc:	single crochet increase
dec:	invisible decrease
sc2tog:	single crochet two together
MR:	magic ring
BLO:	back loops only

Graham the S'more (Continued)

GRAHAM CRACKER

This piece is worked in rows using golden-brown yarn. Repeat the pattern so you have two graham crackers.

R1: Ch 11, then, starting at second chain from the hook, sc 10 (10)

R2–10 : Ch 1, turn, 10 sc (10)

Edge: Ch 1, turn, then working counterclockwise around the piece, 9 sc, 3 sc in corner st, 8 sc, 3 sc in corner st, 8 sc, 3 sc in corner st, 8 sc, 2 sc in last st

Slst in next st. Fasten off, and then weave in the ends with a tapestry needle.

CHOCOLATE

This piece is worked in rows using dark brown yarn.

R1: Ch 9, then starting at second chain from the hook, sc 8 (8)

R2–8: Ch 1, turn, 8 sc (8)

Edge: Ch 1, turn, then working counterclockwise around the piece, 7 sc, 3 sc in corner st, 6 sc, 3 sc in corner st, 6 sc, 3 sc in corner st, 6 sc, 2 sc in last st

Slst in next st. Fasten off, and then weave in the ends with a tapestry needle.

FINISHING

Stack up Graham the S'more's graham cracker, chocolate, marshmallow and another graham cracker and enjoy!

Graham crackers and chocolate, finished

Graham the S'more, finished

SWIRLY
the Soft Serve Ice Cream

My ice cream obsession might be a tad bit out of control, because I created not one, but TWO ice cream patterns for this book. There's always more room for dessert, right? Swirly the Soft Serve Ice Cream is worked in continuous rounds and joins together seamlessly with no sewing necessary. The pattern starts with the cone, leaving a round of free loops to attach the swirl. This pattern calls for white yarn and rainbow sprinkles, but feel free to personalize your ice cream! Swirly's finished size is approximately 6 inches (15.5 cm) tall and 3 inches (8 cm) wide.

CONE

This piece starts at the bottom of the cone using tan yarn.

R1: 6 sc in MR (6)

R2: 1 inc in each st (12)

R3: [1 sc, 1 inc] x6 (18)

R4: Working in BLO, 1 sc in each st (18)

R5–10: 1 sc in each st (18)

R11: Working in FLO, [2 sc, 1 inc] x6 (24)

R12: [3 sc, 1 inc] x6 (30)

R13: Working in BLO, 1 sc in each st (30)

R14–17: 1 sc in each st (30)

R18: Working in FLO, 1 sc in each st (30)

Slst in next st. Fasten off, and then weave in the ends with a tapestry needle.

Place the eyes between R14 and R15, about 4 sc apart. Using black yarn, embroider the mouth onto the front of the face with the tapestry needle, just below the eyes. Add blush for rosy pink cheeks, if you'd like.

ICE CREAM SWIRL

Using white yarn, join the yarn to the first back loop from R18 of the cone.

Ice cream swirl, joining yarn

(CONTINUED)

MATERIALS

0.5 oz tan worsted weight/4-ply yarn

0.5 oz white worsted weight/4-ply yarn

Size E-4 (3.5 mm) crochet hook

Stitch markers

2 (6-mm) black plastic safety eyes

Scrap piece of black yarn for embroidery

Miscellaneous scrap pieces of yarn for embroidery

Polyester fiberfill

Tapestry needle

Cosmetic blush, for adding cheeks (optional)

TERMINOLOGY

R1:	row 1 or round 1
st(s):	stitch(es)
slst:	slip stitch
sc:	single crochet
inc:	single crochet increase
dec:	invisible decrease
MR:	magic ring
FLO:	front loops only
BLO:	back loops only

Swirly the Soft Serve Ice Cream (Continued)

R1: 1 sc in each st (30)

R2: [4 sc, 1 inc] x6 (36)

R3: 1 sc in each (st 36)

R4: [4 sc, 1 dec] x6 (30)

R5: [3 sc, 1 dec] x6 (24)

R6: [2 sc, 1 dec] x6 (18)

R7: Working in FLO, [2 sc, 1 inc] x6 (24)

R8: [3 sc, 1 inc] x6 (30)

R9: [3 sc, 1 dec] x6 (24)

R10: [2 sc, 1 dec] x6 (18)

R11: [1 sc, 1 dec] x6 (12)

R12: Working in FLO, [1 sc, 1 inc] x6 (18)

R13: [2 sc, 1 inc] x6 (24)

R14: [2 sc, 1 dec] x6 (18)

R15: [1 sc, 1 dec] x6 (12)

Embroider different colored sprinkles throughout. Go wild! Stuff the piece with polyester fiberfill.

R16: 6 dec (6)

R17: 3 dec (3)

Close off, and then weave in the ends with a tapestry needle.

Swirly the Soft Serve Ice Cream, finished

IKE
the Ice Cream Scoop

I love all sweets, but words will never begin to describe my love of ice cream. It is my ultimate guilty pleasure. Perfect for good days, bad days, hot days, birthdays or any day of the week ending in the letter "Y", Ike the Ice Cream Scoop is worked in continuous rounds and joins together seamlessly with no sewing necessary. We start with the ice cream scoop, leaving a round of free loops to attach the cone. This pattern calls for pink yarn, but feel free to personalize your scoop! Ike's finished size is approximately 5.5 inches (14 cm) tall and 3 inches (8 cm) wide.

ICE CREAM SCOOP

This piece starts at the top of the scoop using light pink yarn.

R1: 6 sc in MR (6)

R2: 1 inc in each st (12)

R3: [1 sc, 1 inc] x6 (18)

R4: [2 sc, 1 inc] x6 (24)

R5: [3 sc, 1 inc] x6 (30)

R6–12: 1 sc in each st (30)

R13: [3 sc, 1 dec] x6 (24)

R14: Working in FLO, [1 slst, 3 hdc in the next st] x12 (48)

Slst in next st. Fasten off, and then weave in the ends with a tapestry needle.

CONE

Using tan yarn, join the yarn to the first back loop from R14 of the scoop.

R1: 1 sc in each st (24)

R2: [6 sc, 1 dec] x3 (21)

R3: 1 sc in each st (21)

R4: [5 sc, 1 dec] x3 (18)

R5: 1 sc in each st (18)

R6: [4 sc, 1 dec] x3 (15)

R7: 1 sc in each st (15)

Place the eyes between R4 and R5, about 4 sc apart. Using black yarn, embroider the mouth onto the front of the face with the tapestry needle, just below the eyes. Add blush for rosy pink cheeks, if you'd like. Stuff the piece with polyester fiberfill.

R8: [3 sc, 1 dec] x3 (12)

R9: 1 sc in each st (12)

R10: [2 sc, 1 dec] x3 (9)

R11: 1 sc in each st (9)

R12: [1 sc, 1 dec] x3 (6)

Stuff the piece with polyester fiberfill. Close off, and then weave in the ends with a tapestry needle.

Cone, joining yarn

MATERIALS

0.5 oz light pink worsted weight/4-ply yarn

0.5 oz tan worsted weight/4-ply yarn

Size E-4 (3.5 mm) crochet hook

Stitch markers

2 (6-mm) black plastic safety eyes

Scrap piece of black yarn for embroidery

Polyester fiberfill

Tapestry needle

Cosmetic blush, for adding cheeks (optional)

TERMINOLOGY

R1:	row 1 or round 1
st(s):	stitch(es)
slst:	slip stitch
sc:	single crochet
inc:	single crochet increase
dec:	invisible decrease
hdc:	half double crochet
MR:	magic ring
FLO:	front loops only

MACY
the Macaron

I'm obsessed with baking macarons. These sweet treats typically include jam, ganache or buttercream sandwiched between two delectable, melt-in-your-mouth almond cookies. If baking's not your jam, try your hand at a crocheted macaron instead! Macy the Macaron is worked in continuous rounds and joins together seamlessly with no sewing necessary. The techniques used in this pattern are unique and require working in the third loop of the half double crochet, as described below. This pattern calls for pink yarn, but feel free to mix up the colors for an assortment of flavors and display them in a box for maximum cuteness! Macy's finished size is approximately 2 inches (5 cm) tall and 2.5 inches (6.5 cm) wide.

For this pattern, we will be working in the third loop of the half double crochet. Just like a single crochet, the top stitches create a series of V shapes. Behind the Vs, you will see a bar going across the stitch. This is where you will insert your hook and continue to work your stitch as you normally would.

MACARON

This piece starts at the top of the macaron using light pink yarn.

R1: 6 sc in MR (6)

R2: 1 inc in each st (12)

R3: [1 sc, 1 inc] x6 (18)

R4: [2 sc, 1 inc] x6 (24)

R5: 1 sc in each st (24)

R6: 1 hdc in each st (24)

Switch to white yarn.

R7: 1 sc in the third loop of each hdc (24)

Switch to light pink yarn.

R8: 1 hdc in each st (24)

R9: 1 sc in the third loop of each hdc (24)

R10: 1 sc in each st (24)

Place the eyes between R3 and R4, about 6 sc apart. Using black yarn, embroider the mouth onto the front of the face with the tapestry needle, just below the eyes. Add blush for rosy pink cheeks, if you'd like.

R11: [2 sc, 1 dec] x6 (18)

R12: [1 sc, 1 dec] x6 (12)

R13: 6 dec (6)

Stuff the piece with polyester fiberfill. Close off, and then weave in the ends with a tapestry needle.

Macaron, round 7

Iggy
the Eggplant

Contrary to its name, eggplants are neither egg nor vegetable, they are actually berries! But whatever this deceptive plant may be, there is no denying that Iggy's sweet face pairs perfectly with his silly, awkward body. Iggy the Eggplant is worked in continuous rounds and joins together seamlessly with no sewing necessary. The leaves are added on last using a few different stitches to create a series of triangular shapes. Iggy's finished size is approximately 5 inches (13 cm) tall and 2.5 inches (6.5 cm) wide.

MATERIALS

0.5 oz light green worsted weight/4-ply yarn

1 oz light purple worsted weight/4-ply yarn

Size E-4 (3.5 mm) crochet hook

Stitch markers

2 (6-mm) black plastic safety eyes

Scrap piece of black yarn for embroidery

Polyester fiberfill

Tapestry needle

Cosmetic blush, for adding cheeks (optional)

TERMINOLOGY

R1:	row 1 or round 1
st(s):	stitch(es)
slst:	slip stitch
ch:	chain
sc:	single crochet
inc:	single crochet increase
dec:	invisible decrease
hdc:	half double crochet
dc:	double crochet
MR:	magic ring
FLO:	front loops only
BLO:	back loops only

EGGPLANT

This piece starts at the stem of the eggplant using light green yarn.

R1: 6 sc in MR (6)

R2-4: 1 sc in each st (6)

R5: Working in FLO, 1 inc in each st (12)

R6: [1 sc, 1 inc] x6 (18)

R7: [2 sc, 1 inc] x6 (24)

R8: 1 sc in each st (24)

Change to light purple yarn.

R9: Working in BLO, 1 sc in each st (24)

R10 -17: 1 sc in each st (24)

Place the eyes between R13 and R14, about 4 sc apart. Using black yarn, embroider the mouth onto the front of the face with the tapestry needle, just below the eyes. Add blush for rosy pink cheeks, if you'd like.

R18: 11 sc, 1 inc, 7 sc, 1 inc, 4 sc (26)

R19: 1 sc in each st (26)

R20: 12 sc, 1 inc, 8 sc, 1 inc, 4 sc (28)

R21: 1 sc in each st (28)

R22: 13 sc, 1 inc, 9 sc, 1 inc, 4 sc (30)

R23-25: 1 sc in each st (30)

R26: [3 sc, 1 dec] x6 (24)

R27: [2 sc, 1 dec] x6 (18)

R28: [1 sc, 1 dec] x6 (12)

R29: 6 dec (6)

Stuff the piece with polyester fiberfill. Close off, and then weave in the ends with a tapestry needle.

LEAVES

Using light green yarn, join the yarn to the first front loop from R9 of the eggplant.

[1 sc, 1 hdc and 1 dc in next st, ch 1, 1 dc and 1 hdc in next st, 1 sc and 1 slst in next st] x6

Slst in next st. Fasten off, and then weave in the ends with a tapestry needle.

Leaves, joining yarn

AVA
the Avocado

Holy guacamole! Avocados are all the rage. On toast, in guacamole, sliced or diced . . . the possibilities are endless. Make this little guy as the perfect gift for the avocado lovers in your life. Ava the Avocado is worked in continuous rounds and joins together seamlessly with no sewing necessary. To create clean creases and lines when transitioning between components, we will be working in only the front loops or back loops for certain rounds. Ava's finished size is approximately 3.5 inches (9 cm) tall by 3 inches (8 cm) wide.

AVOCADO

This piece starts at the center of the pit using golden-brown yarn.

R1: 6 sc in MR (6)

R2: 1 inc in each st (12)

R3: [1 sc, 1 inc] x6 (18)

R4–5: 1 sc in each st (18)

Switch to lime green yarn.

R6: Working in FLO, [2 sc, 1 inc] x6 (24)

R7: 3 sc, 1 inc, 6 sc, 3 inc, 6 sc, 1 inc, 3 sc, 1 inc (30)

R8: 4 sc, 1 inc, 7 sc, 1 inc, 1 sc, 1 inc, 1 sc, 1 inc, 7 sc, 1 inc, 4 sc, 1 inc (36)

Place the eyes between R2 and R3, about 4 sc apart. Using black yarn, embroider the mouth onto the front of the face with the tapestry needle, just below the eyes. Add blush for rosy pink cheeks, if you'd like.

Switch to dark green yarn.

R9: Working in BLO, 1 sc in each st (36)

R10: 1 sc in each st (36)

R11: 1 sc in each st (36)

R12: 4 sc, 1 dec, 7 sc, 1 dec, 1 sc, 1 dec, 1 sc, 1 dec, 7 sc, 1 dec, 4 sc, 1 dec (30)

R13: 3 sc, 1 dec, 6 sc, 3 dec, 6 sc, 1 dec, 3 sc, 1 dec (24)

R14: [2 sc, 1 dec] x6 (18)

R15: [1 sc, 1 dec] x6 (12)

R16: 6 dec (6)

Stuff the piece with polyester fiberfill. Close off, and then weave in the ends with a tapestry needle.

Ava the Avocado, finished

MATERIALS

0.5 oz golden-brown worsted weight/4-ply yarn

0.5 oz lime green worsted weight/4-ply yarn

0.5 oz dark green worsted weight/4-ply yarn

Size E-4 (3.5 mm) crochet hook

Stitch markers

2 (6-mm) black plastic safety eyes

Scrap piece of black yarn for embroidery

Polyester fiberfill

Tapestry needle

Cosmetic blush, for adding cheeks (optional)

TERMINOLOGY

R1:	row 1 or round 1
st(s):	stitch(es)
sc:	single crochet
inc:	single crochet increase
dec:	invisible decrease
MR:	magic ring
FLO:	front loops only
BLO:	back loops only

WALTER
the Watermelon

I have a confession. As a kid, I wholeheartedly believed that if I ate a watermelon seed, a watermelon would grow in my belly. Thankfully, I know better now and can enjoy this refreshingly sweet treat all summer long. Walter the Watermelon is worked in continuous rounds and joins together seamlessly with no sewing necessary. For this pattern, we work three single crochets at each corner to create the watermelon rind. Then a series of decreases form to give Walter shape. Walter's finished size is approximately 3 inches (8 cm) tall by 3 inches (8 cm) wide by 1.5 inches (4 cm) thick.

SKILL LEVEL

WATERMELON

This piece starts at the watermelon rind using lime green yarn.

R1: Ch 15 to create a foundation chain. Starting at the second chain from the hook, sc 13 in the back loops of the foundation chain. 1 inc the last stitch, rotate the chain, then 1 sc in the front loop of the same stitch. sc 12 in the front loops, 1 inc in the last stitch (30)

R2: 3 sc in next st, 12 sc, 3 sc in next st, 1 sc, 3 sc in next st, 12 sc, 3 sc in next st, 1 sc (38)

R3: Working in BLO, 1 sc in each st (38)

R4: 1 sc, 1 dec, 12 sc, 1 dec, 3 sc, 1 dec, 12 sc, 1 dec, 2 sc (34)

Switch to white yarn.

R5: 1 sc in each st (30)

Switch to flamingo pink yarn.

R6: 1 sc, 1 dec, 10 sc, 1 dec, 3 sc, 1 dec, 10 sc, 1 dec, 2 sc (30)

R7: 1 sc in each st (30)

R8: 1 sc, 1 dec, 8 sc, 1 dec, 3 sc, 1 dec, 8 sc, 1 dec, 2 sc (26)

R9: 1 sc in each st (26)

R10: 1 sc, 1 dec, 6 sc, 1 dec, 3 sc, 1 dec, 6 sc, 1 dec, 2 sc (22)

R11: 1 sc in each st (22)

R12: 2 sc, 1 dec, 4 sc, 1 dec, 3 sc, 1 dec, 4 sc, 1 dec, 1 sc (18)

R13: 1 sc in each st (18)

Place the eyes between R8 and R9, about 4 sc apart. Using black yarn, embroider the mouth onto the front of the face with the tapestry needle, just below the eyes. Add blush for rosy pink cheeks, if you'd like.

R14: 2 sc, 1 dec, 2 sc, 1 dec, 3 sc, 1 dec, 2 sc, 1 dec, 1 sc (14)

R15: 1 sc in each st (14)

R16: 2 sc, 2 dec, 3 sc, 2 dec, 1 sc (10)

R17: 1 sc in each st (10)

R18: 3 sc, 1 dec, 3 sc, 1 dec (8)

Stuff the piece with polyester fiberfill. Stitch along the opening to close off, and then weave in the ends with a tapestry needle.

Watermelon, round 1

MATERIALS

0.5 oz lime green worsted weight/4-ply yarn

0.5 oz white worsted weight/4-ply yarn

0.5 oz flamingo pink worsted weight/4-ply yarn

Size E-4 (3.5 mm) crochet hook

Stitch markers

2 (6-mm) black plastic safety eyes

Scrap piece of black yarn for embroidery

Polyester fiberfill

Tapestry needle

Cosmetic blush, for adding cheeks (optional)

TERMINOLOGY

R1:	row 1 or round 1
st(s):	stitch(es)
ch:	chain
sc:	single crochet
inc:	single crochet increase
dec:	invisible decrease
BLO:	back loops only

CINNA
the Cinnamon Roll

These decadently rich and sticky-sweet pastries are to die for. Just picturing those big, fluffy rolls packed with cinnamon sugar and topped with warm gooey vanilla glaze makes me drool. It's time to get back to work, because we're on a roll! Cinna the Cinnamon Roll is worked in continuous rounds and joins together seamlessly with no sewing necessary. We will be working with two colors at the same time and alternating rounds. Cinna's finished size is approximately 2.5 inches (6.5 cm) tall and 3 inches (8 cm) wide.

SKILL LEVEL

MATERIALS

1 oz golden-brown worsted weight/4-ply yarn

0.5 oz dark brown worsted weight/4-ply yarn

Size E-4 (3.5 mm) crochet hook

Stitch markers

2 (6-mm) black plastic safety eyes

Scrap piece of black yarn for embroidery

Scrap piece of white yarn for embroidery

Polyester fiberfill

Tapestry needle

Cosmetic blush, for adding cheeks (optional)

CINNAMON ROLL

This piece starts at the top of the cinnamon roll using golden-brown yarn.

R1: 6 sc in MR (6)

R2: 1 inc in each st, then place a stitch marker to hold the last stitch (12)

Join the dark brown yarn to the next stitch. For the next few rounds, you will be working with both colors and alternating rounds to create the swirl. Do not cut the yarn when changing colors. Just pick up the marked stitch from the previous round.

R3: Working with the dark brown yarn in BLO, 1 sc in each st, then place a stitch marker to hold the last stitch (12)

Cinnamon roll, joining yarn

Cinnamon roll, round 4

(CONTINUED)

TERMINOLOGY

R1:	row 1 or round 1
st(s):	stitch(es)
sc:	single crochet
inc:	single crochet increase
dec:	invisible decrease
sc2tog:	single crochet two together
MR:	magic ring
FLO:	front loops only
BLO:	back loops only

Cinna the Cinnamon Roll (Continued)

R4: Working with the golden-brown yarn in FLO, [1 sc, 1 inc] x6, then place a stitch marker to hold the last stitch (18)

R5: Working with the dark brown yarn in BLO, 1 sc in each st, then place a stitch marker to hold the last stitch (18)

R6: Working with the golden-brown yarn in FLO, [2 sc, 1 inc] x6, then place a stitch marker to hold the last stitch (24)

R7: Working with the dark brown yarn in BLO, [3 sc, 1 inc] x6, then slst in next st and fasten off (30)

R8: Working with the golden-brown yarn, [4 sc, 1 inc] x6 (36)

Continue with the golden-brown yarn.

R9: Working in BLO, 1 sc in each st (36)

R10 –14: 1 sc in each st (36)

Place the eyes between R11 and R12, about 4 sc apart. Using black yarn, embroider the mouth onto the front of the face with the tapestry needle, just below the eyes. Add blush for rosy pink cheeks, if you'd like. Using white yarn, embroider frosting in a zigzag pattern across the top of the cinnamon roll.

R15: Working in BLO, [4 sc, 1 sc2tog] x6 (30)

R16: [3 sc, 1 dec] x6 (24)

R17: [2 sc, 1 dec] x6 (18)

R18: [1 sc, 1 dec] x6 (12)

R19: 6 dec (6)

Stuff the piece with polyester fiberfill. Close off, and then weave in the ends with a tapestry needle.

Cinnamon roll, round 8

Cinnamon roll, round 15

Cinna the Cinnamon Roll, finished

GOLDIE
the Drumstick

I love fried chicken, but this pattern was actually inspired by my sassy little corgi terrier puppy, Carly! When she sprawls out on the floor in her classic corgi sploot, her stumpy little legs look just like drumsticks. Corgi owners refer to those silly little stumps as drummies! Goldie the Drumstick is worked in continuous rounds and joins together with no sewing necessary. Each side of the bone is made separately and joined together to create a seamless piece. Goldie's finished size is approximately 5 inches (13 cm) tall and 3 inches (8 cm) wide.

BONE PART 1

This piece starts at the tip of the first part of the bone using white yarn.

R1: 6 sc in MR (6)

R2: [1 sc, 1 inc] x3 (9)

Slst in next st. Fasten off, and then weave in the ends with a tapestry needle.

BONE PART 2

This piece starts at the tip of the second part of the bone using white yarn.

R1: 6 sc in MR (6)

R2: [1 sc, 1 inc] x3 (9)

Leave your hook in the last stitch and proceed to the chicken.

CHICKEN

Hold the bone sections together as shown. With the last loop of the bone piece still on your hook, slst 1 through both pieces to join.

To begin the next round, start by crocheting clockwise around both pieces, excluding the slst used to join.

Bone parts 1 and 2, joining

(CONTINUED)

MATERIALS

0.5 oz white worsted weight/4-ply yarn

1 oz golden-brown worsted weight/4-ply yarn

Size E-4 (3.5 mm) crochet hook

Stitch markers

2 (6-mm) black plastic safety eyes

Scrap piece of black yarn for embroidery

Polyester fiberfill

Tapestry needle

Cosmetic blush, for adding cheeks (optional)

TERMINOLOGY

R1:	row 1 or round 1
st(s):	stitch(es)
slst:	slip stitch
sc:	single crochet
inc:	single crochet increase
dec:	invisible decrease
MR:	magic ring

Goldie the Drumstick (Continued)

R1: 1 sc in each st (16)

R2: [2 sc, 1 dec] x4 (12)

R3: [2 sc, 1 dec] x3 (9)

R4: 1 sc in each st (9)

Stuff the piece with polyester fiberfill and switch to golden-brown yarn.

R5: 1 sc in each st (9)

R6: 1 sc in each st (9)

R7: [2 sc, 1 inc] x3 (12)

R8: [3 sc, 1 inc] x3 (15)

R9: [4 sc, 1 inc] x3 (18)

R10: [5 sc, 1 inc] x3 (21)

R11: [6 sc, 1 inc] x3 (24)

R12: [7 sc, 1 inc] x3 (27)

R13: [8 sc, 1 inc] x3 (30)

R14: [9 sc, 1 inc] x3 (33)

R15: [10 sc, 1 inc] x3 (36)

R16–18: 1 sc in each st (36)

Place the eyes between R11 and R12, about 4 sc apart. Using black yarn, embroider the mouth onto the front of the face with the tapestry needle, just below the eyes. Add blush for rosy pink cheeks, if you'd like.

R19: [4 sc, 1 dec] x6 (30)

R20: [3 sc, 1 dec] x6 (24)

R21: [2 sc, 1 dec] x6 (18)

R22: [1 sc, 1 dec] x6 (12)

R23: 6 dec (6)

Stuff the piece with polyester fiberfill. Close off, and then weave in the ends with a tapestry needle.

Chicken, round 1

Goldie the Drumstick, finished

BENTO BOX

A bento box is a home-packed boxed lunch that is typically filled with an assortment of delicious Japanese treats, just like the sushi and dumplings found in this chapter! In some cases, the bento boxes are elaborately arranged and decorated to look like characters, animals, people or plants. An amigurumi version of some of these delightful treats seemed like a no brainer!

In Japan, many children bring these fun and intricate bento boxes to school. However, being fourth generation Japanese-American (Yonsei) meant that much of my culture had been lost over the years. My packed lunches typically consisted of a sandwich, a bag of chips, a juice pouch and a fruit roll-up!

But with strong family roots in Hawaii and a close-knit Japanese-American community, my family has adopted a more casual and diverse take on the Asian American experience and I was exposed to the perfect melting pot of cultures and food. I originally planned to fill this chapter with Japanese cuisine, but ultimately couldn't resist some of the Hawaiian and Chinese treats I've come to love like Sam the Spam Musubi (page 99) and Lucky the Fortune Cookie (page 111)! The designs may not be the most traditional, but they are undeniably adorable!

DANNY
the Dango

These sweet and chewy treats are a festival favorite in Japan. The dumplings are typically made with rice flour, skewered on a stick and enjoyed under the beautiful blooming cherry blossom trees. They are cute, colorful and perfect for amigurumi. Danny the Dango is worked in continuous rounds and joins together seamlessly with no sewing necessary. A series of increases and decreases create the illusion of three separate balls of mochi. Danny's finished size is approximately 6.5 inches (16.5 cm) tall and 2 inches (5 cm) wide.

MATERIALS

0.5 oz light pink worsted weight/4-ply yarn

0.5 oz white worsted weight/4-ply yarn

0.5 oz light green worsted weight/4-ply yarn

0.5 oz tan worsted weight/4-ply yarn

Size E-4 (3.5 mm) crochet hook

2 (6-mm) black plastic safety eyes

Scrap piece of black yarn for embroidery

Polyester fiberfill

Tapestry needle

Cosmetic blush, for adding cheeks (optional)

TERMINOLOGY

R1:	row 1 or round 1
st(s):	stitch(es)
sc:	single crochet
inc:	single crochet increase
dec:	invisible decrease
MR:	magic ring
FLO:	front loops only

DANGO

This piece starts at the top of the dango using light pink yarn.

R1: 6 sc in MR (6)

R2: 1 inc in each st (12)

R3: [1 sc, 1 inc] x6 (18)

R4: [2 sc, 1 inc] x6 (24)

R5–8: 1 sc in each st (24)

R9: [2 sc, 1 dec] x6 (18)

R10: [1 sc, 1 dec] x6 (24)

Stuff the piece with polyester fiberfill. Change to white yarn.

R11: Working in FLO, [1 sc, 1 inc] x6 (18)

R12: [2 sc, 1 inc] x6 (24)

R13–16: 1 sc in each st (24)

R17: [2 sc, 1 dec] x6 (18)

R18: [1 sc, 1 dec] x6 (24)

Place the eyes between R14 and R15, about 4 sc apart. Using black yarn, embroider the mouth onto the front of the face with the tapestry needle, just below the eyes. Add blush for rosy pink cheeks, if you'd like. Stuff the piece with polyester fiberfill.

Change to light green yarn.

R19: Working in FLO, [1 sc, 1 inc] x6 (18)

R20: [2 sc, 1 inc] x6 (24)

R21–24: 1 sc in each st (24)

R25: [2 sc, 1 dec] x6 (18)

R26: [1 sc, 1 dec] x6 (24)

R27: 6 dec (6)

Stuff the piece with polyester fiberfill. Change to tan yarn.

R28–33: 1 sc in each st (6)

Close off, and then weave in the ends with a tapestry needle.

Danny the Dango, finished

SAM
the Spam Musubi

Spam Musubi is a classic Hawaiian snack composed of grilled spam and a block of sticky white rice, wrapped in seaweed. Before every family get-together, my siblings and I would slave away at the spam musubi assembly line. But making these snacks always marked the start of a day filled with family, love and laughter. For me, spam musubi is the ultimate comfort food. Sam the Spam Musubi is composed of three separate pieces that stack together to create this onolicious (delicious) snack. For this pattern, we work three single crochets at each corner to create the rectangular shape. Then the seaweed piece wraps around the spam and rice to hold everything together. Sam's finished size is approximately 4.5 inches (11.5 cm) long, 2 inches (5 cm) wide and 1.5 inches (4 cm) thick.

SPAM

This piece starts at the center of the spam using flamingo pink yarn.

R1: Ch 10 to create a foundation chain. Starting at the second chain from the hook, sc 9 in the back loops of the foundation chain. Rotate the chain, then sc 9 in the front loops (18)

R2: 3 sc in next st, 7 sc, 3 sc in next st, 3 sc in next st, 7 sc, 3 sc in next st (26)

R3: 1 sc, 3 sc in next st, 9 sc, 3 sc in next st, 2 sc, 3 sc in next st, 9 sc, 3 sc in next st, 1 sc (34)

R4: 2 sc, 3 sc in next st, 11 sc, 3 sc in next st, 4 sc, 3 sc in next st, 11 sc, 3 sc in next st, 2 sc (42)

R5: 3 sc, 3 sc in next st, 13 sc, 3 sc in next st, 6 sc, 3 sc in next st, 13 sc, 3 sc in next st, 3 sc (50)

R6: Working in BLO, 1 sc in each st (50)

Spam, round 1

(CONTINUED)

R7: Working in BLO, 3 sc, sc next 3 sts together, 13 sc, sc next 3 sts together, 6 sc, sc next 3 sts together, 13 sc, sc next 3 sts together, 3 sc (42)

R8: 2 sc, sc next 3 sts together, 11 sc, sc next 3 sts together, 4 sc, sc next 3 sts together, 11 sc, sc next 3 sts together, 2 sc (34)

R9: 1 sc, sc next 3 sts together, 9 sc, sc next 3 sts together, 2 sc, sc next 3 sts together, 9 sc, sc next 3 sts together, 1 sc (26)

R10: Sc next 3 sts together, 7 sc, sc next 3 sts together, sc next 3 sts together, 7 sc, sc next 3 sts together (18)

No stuffing necessary. Stitch along the opening to close off, and then weave in the ends with a tapestry needle.

RICE

This piece starts at the center of the rice using white yarn.

R1: Ch 10 to create a foundation chain. Starting at the second chain from the hook, sc 9 in the back loops of the foundation chain. Rotate the chain, then sc 9 in the front loops (18)

R2: 3 sc in next st, 7 sc, 3 sc in next st, 3 sc in next st, 7 sc, 3 sc in next st (26)

R3: 1 sc, 3 sc in next st, 9 sc, 3 sc in next st, 2 sc, 3 sc in next st, 9 sc, 3 sc in next st, 1 sc (34)

R4: 2 sc, 3 sc in next st, 11 sc, 3 sc in next st, 4 sc, 3 sc in next st, 11 sc, 3 sc in next st, 2 sc (42)

R5: 3 sc, 3 sc in next st, 13 sc, 3 sc in next st, 6 sc, 3 sc in next st, 13 sc, 3 sc in next st, 3 sc (50)

R6: Working in BLO, 1 sc in each st (50)

R7-9: 1 sc in each st (50)

Place the eyes between R7 and R8, about 4 sc apart. Using black yarn, embroider the mouth onto the front of the face with the tapestry needle, just below the eyes. Add blush for rosy pink cheeks, if you'd like.

R10: Working in BLO, 3 sc, sc next 3 sts together, 13 sc, sc next 3 sts together, 6 sc, sc next 3 sts together, 13 sc, sc next 3 sts together, 3 sc (42)

R11: 2 sc, sc next 3 sts together, 11 sc, sc next 3 sts together, 4 sc, sc next 3 sts together, 11 sc, sc next 3 sts together, 2 sc (34)

R12: 1 sc, sc next 3 sts together, 9 sc, sc next 3 sts together, 2 sc, sc next 3 sts together, 9 sc, sc next 3 sts together, 1 sc (26)

R13: Sc next 3 sts together, 7 sc, sc next 3 sts together, sc next 3 sts together, 7 sc, sc next 3 sts together (18)

Stuff the piece with polyester fiberfill. Stitch along the opening to close off, and then weave in the ends with a tapestry needle.

SEAWEED

Using black yarn, we will form a chain into a circle and continue the work. This allows us to work in continuous rounds and create a seamless piece.

R1: Ch 30, then form the chain into a circle (be careful not to twist the work). Starting in the first chain, 1 sc in each st (30)

R2-4: 1 sc in each st (30)

Slst in the next st. Fasten off, and then weave in the ends with a tapestry needle.

FINISHING

Stack up the rice and spam, slide on the seaweed piece and you're all pau! (All done!)

Spam, finished

Rice, finished

Seaweed, round 1

Seaweed, finished

Sam the Spam Musubi, finished

EʙI
the Shrimp Nigiri

Nigiri is another form of sushi with thinly sliced fish placed over seasoned rice. Making these delicious delicacies is something of an artform. What better way to re-create them than with another form of artistry, crochet! Ebi the Nigiri is worked in continuous rounds. She is composed of two separate pieces that stack together. The shrimp is made with alternating colors to create stripes, then we use a series of double crochets to shape the tail. Ebi's finished size is approximately 3 inches (9 cm) tall, 2 inches (5 cm) wide and 2 inches (5 cm) long.

RICE

This piece uses white yarn and starts at the top of the rice using a foundation chain to create an oval.

R1: Ch 7 to create a foundation chain. Starting at the second chain from the hook, sc 5 in the back loops of the foundation chain. 1 inc in the last stitch, rotate the chain, then 1 sc in the front loop of the same stitch. sc 4 in the front loops, 1 inc in last stitch (18)

R2: 1 inc, 4 sc, 3 inc, 4 sc, 2 inc (24)

R3: 1 sc, 1 inc, 5 sc, 1 inc, 1 sc, 1 inc, 1 sc, 1 inc, 5 sc, 1 inc, 1 sc, 1 inc (30)

R4: 2 sc, 1 inc, 6 sc, 1 inc, 2 sc, 1 inc, 2 sc, 1 inc, 6 sc, 1 inc, 2 sc, 1 inc (36)

R5-6: 1 sc in each st (36)

R7: 2 sc, 1 dec, 6 sc, 1 dec, 2 sc, 1 dec, 2 sc, 1 dec, 6 sc, 1 dec, 2 sc, 1 dec (30)

R8: 1 sc, 1 dec, 5 sc, 1 dec, 1 sc, 1 dec, 1 sc, 1 dec, 5 sc, 1 dec, 1 sc, 1 dec (24)

R9: 1 dec, 4 sc, 3 dec, 4 sc, 2 dec (18)

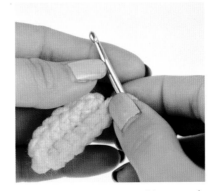

Rice, round 1

(CONTINUED)

SKILL LEVEL

MATERIALS

0.5 oz white worsted weight/4-ply yarn

0.5 oz orange worsted weight/ 4-ply yarn

Size E-4 (3.5 mm) crochet hook

Stitch markers

2 (6-mm) black plastic safety eyes

Scrap piece of black yarn for embroidery

Scrap piece of orange yarn for embroidery

Polyester fiberfill

Tapestry needle

Cosmetic blush, for adding cheeks (optional)

TERMINOLOGY

R1:	row 1 or round 1
st(s):	stitch(es)
slst:	slip stitch
ch:	chain
sc:	single crochet
inc:	single crochet increase
dec:	invisible decrease
dc:	double crochet
MR:	magic ring

Ebi the Shrimp Nigiri (Continued)

Place the eyes between R5 and R6, about 4 sc apart. Using black yarn, embroider the mouth onto the front of the face with the tapestry needle, just below the eyes. Add blush for rosy pink cheeks, if you'd like. Stuff the piece with polyester fiberfill. Stitch along the opening to close off, and then weave in the ends with a tapestry needle.

SHRIMP

This piece starts at the front of the shrimp using orange yarn.

R1: 6 sc in MR (6)

R2: Using white yarn, 1 inc in each st (12)

R3: Using orange yarn, [1 sc, 1 inc] x6 (18)

R4: Using white yarn, 1 sc in each st (18)

R5: Using orange yarn, 1 sc in each st (18)

R6: Using white yarn, [4 sc, 1 dec] x3 (15)

R7: Using orange yarn, 1 sc in each st (15)

R8: Using white yarn, 1 sc in each st (15)

R9: Using orange yarn, [3 sc, 1 dec] x3 (12)

R10: Using white yarn, 1 sc in each st (12)

R11: Using orange yarn, [2 sc, 1 dec] x3 (9)

R12: Using white yarn, [1 sc, 1 dec] x3 (6)

Switch to orange yarn. Flatten the piece.

R13: Ch 1, turn, then working through the front and back stitches, sc 3 (3)

R14: Ch 1, turn, then 5 dc in first st, 1 slst in next st, 5 dc in next st, 1 slst in same st

No stuffing necessary. Fasten off and weave in the ends with a tapestry needle. Using orange yarn, embroider one long line along the top of the shrimp going from the tail to the tip of the shrimp. Add a stitch connecting the shrimp to the rice, if you'd like.

Rice, finished

Shrimp, round 13

Shrimp, finished

Ebi the Shrimp Nigiri, finished

peppy
the Hot Sauce

Spice up your life with this sassy little bottle of hot sauce. He'll be sure to put a little pep in your step, stride in your glide and move in your groove! Now get crocheting, hot stuff! Peppy the Hot Sauce is worked in continuous rounds and joins together seamlessly with no sewing necessary. To create clean creases and lines when transitioning between components, we will be working in only the front loops or back loops for certain rounds. Peppy's finished size is approximately 6 inches (15.5 cm) tall and 3 inches (8 cm) wide.

HOT SAUCE

This piece starts at the bottom of the bottle using red yarn.

R1: 6 sc in MR (6)

R2: 1 inc in each st (12)

R3: [1 sc, 1 inc] x6 (18)

R4: [2 sc, 1 inc] x6 (24)

R5: [3 sc, 1 inc] x6 (30)

R6: Working in BLO, 1 sc in each st (30)

R7–19: 1 sc in each st (30)

Place the eyes between R11 and R12, about 4 sc apart. Using black yarn, embroider the mouth onto the front of the face with the tapestry needle, just below the eyes.

R20: [3 sc, 1 dec] x6 (24)

R21: [2 sc, 1 dec] x6 (18)

R22: [1 sc, 1 dec] x6 (12)

R23: 1 sc in each st (12)

Stuff the piece with polyester fiberfill. Switch to lime green yarn.

R24: Working in FLO, [3 sc, 1 inc] x3 (15)

R25: Working in BLO, 1 sc in each st (15)

R26: 1 sc in each st (15)

R27: Working in BLO, [3 sc, 1 sc2tog] x3 (12)

R28: 6 dec (6)

Stuff the piece with polyester fiberfill.

R29: Working in FLO, 1 sc in each st (6)

R30: 1 sc in each st (6)

Close off, and then weave in the ends with a tapestry needle.

Peppy the Hot Sauce, finished

SKILL LEVEL

MATERIALS

1 oz red worsted weight/4-ply yarn

0.5 oz lime green worsted weight/4-ply yarn

Size E-4 (3.5 mm) crochet hook

Stitch markers

2 (6-mm) black plastic safety eyes

Scrap piece of black yarn for embroidery

Polyester fiberfill

Tapestry needle

TERMINOLOGY

R1:	row 1 or round 1
st(s):	stitch(es)
sc:	single crochet
inc:	single crochet increase
dec:	invisible decrease
MR:	magic ring
sc2tog:	single crochet two together
FLO:	front loops only
BLO:	back loops only

KIKO
the Soy Sauce

This versatile condiment is a staple in every Asian kitchen and adds depth and flavor to almost any dish. Kiko will pair perfectly with Suki the Sushi Roll (page 113) or Duke the Dumpling (page 115). Kiko the Soy Sauce is worked in continuous rounds and joins together seamlessly with no sewing necessary. A few color changes and increases give this piece its classic look. Kiko's finished size is approximately 4.5 inches (11.5 cm) tall and 3 inches (8 cm) wide.

SOY SAUCE

This piece starts at the bottom of the bottle using black yarn.

R1 : 6 sc in MR (6)

R2 : 1 inc in each st (12)

R3 : [1 sc, 1 inc] x6 (18)

R4 : [2 sc, 1 inc] x6 (24)

R5 : [3 sc, 1 inc] x6 (30)

R6 : [4 sc, 1 inc] x6 (36)

R7 : Working in BLO, 1 sc in each st (36)

R8 : 1 sc in each st (36)

R9 : 1 sc in each st (36)

R10 : [10 sc, 1 dec] x3 (33)

R11 : [9 sc, 1 dec] x3 (30)

R12 : [8 sc, 1 dec] x3 (27)

R13 : [7 sc, 1 dec] x3 (24)

Change to white yarn.

R14 : [6 sc, 1 dec] x3 (21)

R15 : [5 sc, 1 dec] x3 (18)

R16 : [4 sc, 1 dec] x3 (15)

R17 : [3 sc, 1 dec] x3 (12)

R18 : 1 sc in each st (12)

R19 : 1 sc in each st (12)

R20 : [3 sc, 1 inc] x3 (15)

R21 : [4 sc, 1 inc] x3 (18)

R22 : [5 sc, 1 inc] x3 (21)

Place the eyes between R14 and R15, about 4 sc apart. Using black yarn, embroider the mouth onto the front of the face with the tapestry needle, just below the eyes. Add blush for rosy pink cheeks, if you'd like. Stuff the piece with polyester fiberfill.

Change to red yarn.

R23 : Working in BLO, [6 sc, 1 inc] x3 (24)

R24 : [7 sc, 1 inc] x3 (27)

R25 : 7 sc, 3 inc, 7 sc, 1 inc, 8 sc, 1 inc (32)

R26 : 3 sc, 1 dec, 2 sc, 3 dec, 2 sc, 1 dec, [3 sc, 1 dec] x3 (24)

R27 : [2 sc, 1 dec] x6 (18)

R28 : [1 sc, 1 dec] x6 (12)

R29 : 6 dec (6)

Stuff the piece with polyester fiberfill. Close off, and then weave in the ends with a tapestry needle.

Lucky

the Fortune Cookie

Fortune cookies are sweet and delicious, and this amigurumi version is a great way to wish your loved ones "good luck" or to let that special someone know just how lucky they make you feel. Lucky the Fortune Cookie is worked in continuous rounds and joins together seamlessly with no sewing necessary. The cookie starts as a circle, which is folded in half, stuffed and pinched together to give it shape. Lucky's finished size is approximately 3 inches (8 cm) wide, 2 inches (5 cm) tall and 1.5 inches (4 cm) thick.

FORTUNE COOKIE

This piece starts at the center of the fortune cookie using tan yarn.

R1: 6 sc in MR (6)

R2: 1 inc in each st (12)

R3: [1 sc, 1 inc] x6 (18)

R4: [2 sc, 1 inc] x6 (24)

R5: [3 sc, 1 inc] x6 (30)

R6: [4 sc, 1 inc] x6 (36)

R7: [5 sc, 1 inc] x6 (42)

R8: [6 sc, 1 inc] x6 (48)

Place the eyes onto the top quarter of the circle. Using black yarn, embroider the mouth onto the front of the face with the tapestry needle, just below the eyes. Add blush for rosy pink cheeks, if you'd like. Fold the piece in half.

R9: Ch 1, then working through the front and back stitches and stuffing periodically, sc 24 (24)

Ch 1 then fasten off. Weave in the ends with a tapestry needle.

FINISHING

Pinch the piece to create a classic fortune cookie shape. Using a scrap piece of tan yarn and a tapestry needle, run a stitch between R4 and R5 where the two sides of the folded cookie touch. Pull the yarn tight and tie the yarn into a knot to hold the shape. Weave in the ends with a tapestry needle.

Fortune cookie, round 9

Lucky the Fortune Cookie, finished

MATERIALS

0.5 oz tan worsted weight/4-ply yarn

Size E-4 (3.5 mm) crochet hook

Stitch markers

2 (6-mm) black plastic safety eyes

Scrap piece of black yarn for embroidery

Scrap piece of tan yarn for embroidery

Polyester fiberfill

Tapestry needle

Cosmetic blush, for adding cheeks (optional)

TERMINOLOGY

R1:   row 1 or round 1

st(s):   stitch(es)

ch: chain

sc: single crochet

inc: single crochet increase

MR: magic ring

SUKI

the Sushi Roll

Sushi rolls—fresh fish and veggies, covered in seasoned rice and wrapped in seaweed—are probably one of the most iconic Japanese dishes. Sushi chefs train for years to perfect their craft. Luckily, perfecting Suki the Sushi Roll will take much less time. She's adorable, cuddly and beginner friendly! Suki the Sushi Roll is worked in continuous rounds and joins together seamlessly with no sewing necessary. The filling is created with a series of color changes in the first couple rounds. Suki's finished size is approximately 2.5 inches (6.5 cm) tall and 1.5 inches (4 cm) wide.

SUSHI

This piece starts at the center of the sushi roll using light pink yarn.

R1: 6 sc in MR (6)

R2: Continuing with pink yarn, 1 inc. Changing to yellow yarn, 2 inc. Changing to green yarn, 3 inc (12)

Change to white yarn.

R3: [1 sc, 1 inc] x6 (18)

R4: [2 sc, 1 inc] x6 (24)

R5: [3 sc, 1 inc] x6 (30)

R6: [4 sc, 1 inc] x6 (36)

R7: [5 sc, 1 inc] x6 (42)

Place the eyes between R5 and R6, about 6 sc apart. Using black yarn, embroider the mouth onto the front of the face with the tapestry needle, just below the eyes. Add blush for rosy pink cheeks, if you'd like.

Change to black yarn.

R8: Working in BLO, 1 sc in each st (42)

R9: 1 sc in each st (42)

R10: 1 sc in each st (42)

R11: 1 sc in each st (42)

Change to white yarn.

R12: Working in BLO, [5 sc, 1 sc2tog] x6 (36)

R13: [4 sc, 1 dec] x6 (30)

R14: [3 sc, 1 dec] x6 (24)

R15: [2 sc, 1 dec] x6 (18)

R16: [1 sc, 1 dec] x6 (12)

R17: 6 dec (6)

Stuff the piece with polyester fiberfill. Close off, and then weave in the ends with a tapestry needle.

Suki the Sushi Roll, finished

MATERIALS

Scrap piece of light pink worsted weight/4-ply yarn

Scrap piece of yellow worsted weight/4-ply yarn

Scrap piece of light green worsted weight/4-ply yarn

0.5 oz white worsted weight/4-ply yarn

0.5 oz black worsted weight/4-ply yarn

Size E-4 (3.5 mm) crochet hook

Stitch markers

2 (6-mm) black plastic safety eyes

Scrap piece of black yarn for embroidery

Polyester fiberfill

Tapestry needle

Cosmetic blush, for adding cheeks (optional)

TERMINOLOGY

R1:	row 1 or round 1
st(s):	stitch(es)
sc:	single crochet
inc:	single crochet increase
dec:	invisible decrease
sc2tog:	single crochet two together
MR:	magic ring
BLO:	back loops only

SIP SIP HOORAY!

After those last couple of chapters, jam-packed with sweet treats and savory bites, we'll need something refreshing to wash it all down. This chapter is filled with an assortment of drinks to quench everyone's thirst, from an adorable milk carton (page 133) to a tall glass of red wine (page 123). They will pair perfectly with all of your other creations.

Just like their food counterparts, drinks are often used to commemorate a special moment. We clink our glasses together and celebrate life, well wishes, good fortune, friendship and any number of moments, big and small. These celebratory toasts are typically reserved for alcoholic beverages, but there are so many special memories connected to every design in this chapter. Whether the drink reminds you of a moment from your childhood, helps to relieve stress or gives you the fuel you need to make it through the day, there's something for everyone.

So, pick up your glass, carton, teacup or bottle—and cheers to YOU! You are the artists and makers of this world and what you do is so important! You dream, create and inspire everyone around you, and I am honored to be a part of such an amazing community of makers and movers. Thank you for all that you do!

CaTHy
the Coffee Pot

For many of us, life begins after coffee, so I knew a simple coffee cup wouldn't do the trick. When you are stressed, blessed and coffee obsessed, you obviously need the whole pot! Cathy the Coffee Pot is worked in continuous rounds and joins together seamlessly with no sewing necessary. The handle is made first and worked into the coffee pot. As we work on the coffee pot, we leave a round of free loops to attach the spout. Cathy's finished size is approximately 4 inches (10 cm) tall, 4.5 inches (11.5 cm) wide and 4 inches (10 cm) thick.

MATERIALS

0.5 oz red worsted weight/4-ply yarn

0.5 oz dark brown worsted weight/4-ply yarn

0.5 oz white worsted weight/4-ply yarn

Size E-4 (3.5 mm) crochet hook

Stitch markers

2 (6-mm) black plastic safety eyes

Scrap piece of black yarn for embroidery

Polyester fiberfill

Tapestry needle

Cosmetic blush, for adding cheeks (optional)

HANDLE

This piece starts at one end of the handle using red yarn.

R1: Ch 4, then starting at second chain from the hook, sc 3 (3)

In the next round, we will transition from working in rows, to working in rounds. This will be achieved by working clockwise around the front and back loops.

R2: Ch 1, turn, then working in FLO, sc 3. Turn, then working in unworked loops, sc 3 (6)

R3–14: 1 sc in each st (6)

Flatten the piece.

R15: Ch 1, turn, then working through the front and back stitches, sc 3 (3)

Ch 1 then fasten off. No need to weave in the ends, the yarn will end up inside the piece.

Handle, round 2

Handle, finished

(CONTINUED)

TERMINOLOGY

R1:	row 1 or round 1
st(s):	stitch(es)
slst:	slip stitch
ch:	chain
sc:	single crochet
inc:	single crochet increase
dec:	invisible decrease
sc2tog:	single crochet two together
MR:	magic ring
FLO:	front loops only
BLO:	back loops only

Cathy the Coffee Pot (Continued)

COFFEE POT

This piece starts at the bottom of the coffee pot using red yarn.

R1: 6 sc in MR (6)

R2: 1 inc in each st (12)

R3: [1 sc, 1 inc] x6 (18)

R4: [2 sc, 1 inc] x6 (24)

R5: [3 sc, 1 inc] x6 (30)

R6: Working in BLO, [8 sc, 1 dec] x3 (27)

R7: [7 sc, 1 dec] x2, 2 sc, then working though the handle and pot together, sc 3. 2 sc, 1 dec (24)

Switch to dark brown yarn.

R8: Working in FLO, [3 sc, 1 inc] x6 (30)

R9: [4 sc, 1 inc] x6 (36)

R10: [5 sc, 1 inc] x6 (42)

R11–13: 1 sc in each st (42)

Switch to white yarn.

R14: 1 sc in each st (42)

R15: 1 sc in each st (42)

R16: [5 sc, 1 dec] x6 (36)

R17: [4 sc, 1 dec] x6 (30)

R18: [3 sc, 1 dec] x6 (24)

Place the eyes between R15 and R16, about 4 sc apart. Using black yarn, embroider the mouth onto the front of the face with the tapestry needle, just below the eyes. Add blush for rosy pink cheeks, if you'd like.

Switch to red yarn.

R19: 21 sc, then working though the handle and pot together, sc 3 (24)

R20: 1 sc in each st (24)

Switch to white yarn.

R21: Working in BLO, [2 sc, 1 sc2tog] x6 (18)

R22: [1 sc, 1 dec] x6 (12)

R23: 6 dec (6)

Stuff the piece with polyester fiberfill. Close off, and then weave in the ends with a tapestry needle.

SPOUT

Using red yarn, join the yarn to the first front loop from R21 of the coffee pot.

R1: 9 sc, 3 inc, 12 sc (27)

R2: 10 sc, 1 inc, 1 sc, 1 inc, 1 sc, 1 inc, 12 sc (30)

Slst in the next st. Fasten off, and then weave in the ends with a tapestry needle.

Cathy the Coffee Pot, finished

Coffee pot, round 7

Coffee pot, round 19

Coffee pot, finished

Spout, joining yarn

VINNY
the Wine Glass

This book is full of fun, sweet, family-friendly patterns—but sometimes the adults need a little something too. Meet Vinny the Wine Glass. Perfect for winding down after a tough day at the office. Disclaimer: More than a few glasses of wine were consumed in the making of this book. Vinny the Wine Glass is worked in continuous rounds and joins together seamlessly with no sewing necessary! I use a deep red yarn to make a cabernet (my favorite). But if a rosé is more your style, try pink yarn as your main color. Keep your stitches tight or place a straw in the stem of the wine glass to help him stay standing. Vinny stands about 6 inches (15.5 cm) tall and 3 inches (8 cm) wide.

WINE GLASS

This piece starts at the bottom of the wine glass using white yarn.

R1: 6 sc in MR (6)

R2: 1 inc in each st (12)

R3: [1 sc, 1 inc] x6 (18)

R4: [2 sc, 1 inc] x6 (24)

R5: [3 sc, 1 inc] x6 (30)

R6: [4 sc, 1 inc] x6 (36)

R7: Working in BLO, 1 sc in each st (36)

R8: [4 sc, 1 dec] x6 (30)

R9: [3 sc, 1 dec] x6 (24)

R10: [2 sc, 1 dec] x6 (18)

R11: [1 sc, 1 dec] x6 (12)

R12: [2 sc, 1 dec] x3 (9)

R13–20: 1 sc in each st (9)

R21: [2 sc, 1 inc] x3 (12)

Stuff the stem with polyester fiberfill leaving the base empty. Use a straw for extra support (optional). Switch to wine-red yarn.

R22: [1 sc, 1 inc] x6 (18)

R23: [2 sc, 1 inc] x6 (24)

R24: [3 sc, 1 inc] x6 (30)

R25: [4 sc, 1 inc] x6 (36)

R26–27: 1 sc in each st (36)

R28: [10 sc, 1 dec] x3 (33)

R29: 1 sc in each st (33)

R30: [9 sc, 1 dec] x3 (30)

Place the eyes between R27 and R28, about 4 sc apart. Using black yarn, embroider the mouth onto the front of the face with the tapestry needle, just below the eyes.

Switch to white yarn.

R31: 1 sc in each st (30)

R32: [8 sc, 1 dec] x3 (27)

R33: 1 sc in each st (27)

R34: [7 sc, 1 dec] x3 (24)

R35: 1 sc in each st (24)

R36: Working in BLO, [2 sc, 1 sc2tog] x6 (18)

R37: [1 sc, 1 dec] x6 (12)

R38: 6 dec (6)

Stuff the piece with polyester fiberfill. Close off, and then weave in the ends with a tapestry needle.

MATERIALS

1 oz white worsted weight/4-ply yarn

0.5 oz wine-red worsted weight/4-ply yarn

Size E-4 (3.5 mm) crochet hook

Stitch markers

2 (6-mm) black plastic safety eyes

Scrap piece of black yarn for embroidery

Polyester fiberfill

Tapestry needle

Drinking straw (optional)

TERMINOLOGY

R1:	row 1 or round 1
st(s):	stitch(es)
sc:	single crochet
inc:	single crochet increase
dec:	invisible decrease
sc2tog:	single crochet two together
MR:	magic ring
BLO:	back loops only

Tammy
the Teapot

If you're in hot water, there is nothing better to help de-stress than a calming cup of tea. Pour in some water, drop in your tea leaves and turn up the heat. Then just wait for this short and stout little teapot to sing! Tammy the Teapot is worked in continuous rounds and joins together seamlessly with no sewing necessary. The techniques used in this pattern are more advanced and require working in free loops to give Tammy her unique shape. This pattern calls for light purple yarn, but feel free to personalize your teapot with your favorite colors! Tammy's finished size is approximately 3 inches (8 cm) tall, 6 inches (15.5 cm) wide and 4 inches (10 cm) thick.

MATERIALS

1.5 oz light purple worsted weight/4-ply yarn

Size E-4 (3.5 mm) crochet hook

Stitch markers

2 (6-mm) black plastic safety eyes

Scrap piece of black yarn for embroidery

Polyester fiberfill

Tapestry needle

Cosmetic blush, for adding cheeks (optional)

HANDLE

This piece starts at one end of the handle using light purple yarn.

R1: Ch 4, then starting at second chain from the hook, sc 3 (3)

In the next round, we will transition from working in rows, to working in rounds. This will be achieved by working clockwise around the front and back loops.

R2: Ch 1, turn, then working in FLO, sc 3. Turn, then working in unworked loops, sc 3 (6)

R3–12: 1 sc in each st (6)

Flatten the piece.

R13: Ch 1, turn, then working through the front and back stitches, sc 3 (3)

Ch 1 then fasten off. No need to weave in the ends, the yarn will end up inside the piece.

Handle, round 2

Handle, round 13

TERMINOLOGY

R1:	row 1 or round 1
st(s):	stitch(es)
slst:	slip stitch
ch:	chain
sc:	single crochet
inc:	single crochet increase
dec:	invisible decrease
sc2tog:	single crochet two together
MR:	magic ring
FLO:	front loops only
BLO:	back loops only

(CONTINUED)

Tammy the Teapot (Continued)

TEAPOT

This piece starts at the bottom of the pot using light purple yarn.

R1: 6 sc in MR (6)

R2: 1 inc in each st (12)

R3: [1 sc, 1 inc] x6 (18)

R4: [2 sc, 1 inc] x6 (24)

R5: [3 sc, 1 inc] x6 (30)

R6: [4 sc, 1 inc] x6 (36)

R7: Working in BLO, 1 sc in each st (36)

R8: 5 sc, 1 inc, 1 sc, then working though the handle and the pot, sc 3. 1 sc, 1 inc, [5 sc, 1 inc] x2, 2 sc, 1 inc, 2 sc, 1 inc, 5 sc, 1 inc (43)

R9: [6 sc, 1 inc] x4, 3 sc, 1 inc, 3 sc, 1 inc, 6 sc, 1 inc (50)

R10: [7 sc, 1 inc] x4, 4 sc, 1 inc, 4 sc, 1 inc, 7 sc, 1 inc (57)

R11: 1 sc in each st (57)

R12: 36 sc, ch 6 (skip 9 sc for the spout), 12 sc (54)

R13: 1 sc in each st (54)

R14: 1 sc in each st (54)

R15: [7 sc, 1 dec] x6 (48)

R16: 6 sc, 1 dec, 2 sc, then working through the handle and pot, sc 3, 1 sc, 1 dec, [6 sc, 1 dec] x4 (42)

R17: [5 sc, 1 dec] x6 (36)

R18: Working in FLO, 1 sc in each st (36)

Slst in the next st. Fasten off, and then weave in the ends with a tapestry needle. Place the eyes between R11 and R12, about 6 sc apart. Using black yarn, embroider the mouth just below the eyes. Add blush for rosy pink cheeks, if you'd like.

TOP

Using light purple yarn, join the yarn to the first back loop from R18 of the pot.

R1: [4 sc, 1 sc2tog] x6 (30)

R2: [3 sc, 1 dec] x6 (24)

R3: [2 sc, 1 dec] x6 (18)

R4: [1 sc, 1 dec] x6 (12)

Stuff the piece with polyester fiberfill.

R5: 6 dec (6)

R6: 1 inc in each st (12)

R7: 6 dec (6)

Close off, and then weave in the ends with a tapestry needle.

SPOUT

Going clockwise, rejoin the light purple yarn at the leg of the sc adjacent to the end of the spout chain.

R1: Using the leg of the adjacent sc and the first stitch of the pot, 1 dec, 8 sc (of the teapot), 6 sc (of the spout chain) (15)

R2: 4 sc, 1 dec, 9 sc (14)

R3: 3 sc, 1 dec, 9 sc (13)

R4: 3 sc, 1 dec, 8 sc (12)

R5: 2 sc, 1 dec, 8 sc (11)

R6: 2 sc, 1 dec, 7 sc (10)

R7: 1 sc in each st (10)

R8: 1 sc in each st (10)

Stuff the piece with polyester fiberfill.

R9: Working in BLO, 5 sc2tog (5)

Close off, and then weave in the ends with a tapestry needle.

Teapot, round 8

Teapot, round 12

Teapot, round 16

Top, joining yarn

Spout, round 1

Tammy the Teapot, finished

Timmy
the Teacup

Pair this dainty little teacup with some crumpets and scones and we've got ourselves a tea party fit for a queen. Pinkies up, this is a posh affair! Timmy the Teacup is worked in continuous rounds and joins together seamlessly with no sewing necessary. The handle is made first and worked into the cup to avoid the guesswork of sewing. This pattern calls for pink yarn, but feel free to personalize your teacup! Timmy's finished size is approximately 3.5 inches (9 cm) wide and 2 inches (5 cm) tall.

HANDLE

This piece starts at one end of the handle using light pink yarn.

R1: Ch 4, then starting at second chain from the hook, sc 3 (3)

In the next round, we will transition from working in rows, to working in rounds. This will be achieved by working clockwise around the front and back loops.

R2: Ch 1, turn, then working in FLO, sc 3, turn, then working in unworked loops, sc 3(6)

R3–10 : 1 sc in each st (6)

Flatten the piece.

R11: Ch 1, turn, then working through the front and back stitches, sc 3 (3)

Ch 1 then fasten off. No need to weave in the ends, the yarn will end up inside the piece.

Handle, round 2

Handle, finished

(CONTINUED)

MATERIALS

0.5 oz light pink worsted weight/4-ply yarn

0.5 oz golden-brown worsted weight/4-ply yarn

Size E-4 (3.5 mm) crochet hook

Stitch markers

2 (6-mm) black plastic safety eyes

Scrap piece of black yarn for embroidery

Polyester fiberfill

Tapestry needle

Cosmetic blush, for adding cheeks (optional)

TERMINOLOGY

R1:	row 1 or round 1
st(s):	stitch(es)
slst:	slip stitch
ch:	chain
sc:	single crochet
inc:	single crochet increase
dec:	invisible decrease
sc2tog:	single crochet two together
MR:	magic ring
FLO:	front loops only
BLO:	back loops only

Timmy the Teacup (Continued)

CUP

This piece starts at the bottom of the cup using light pink yarn.

R1: 6 sc in MR (6)

R2: 1 inc in each st (12)

R3: [1 sc, 1 inc] x6 (18)

R4: [2 sc, 1 inc] x6 (24)

R5: Working in BLO, 1 sc in each st (24)

R6: 3 sc, 1 inc, then working through the handle and cup, sc 3. 1 inc, [3 sc, 1 inc] x4 (30)

R7: [9 sc, 1 inc] x3 (33)

R8: [10 sc, 1 inc] x3 (36)

R9: 1 sc in each st (36)

R10: 1 sc in each st (36)

R11: 6 sc, then working through the handle and cup, sc 3. 27 sc (36)

R12: 1 sc in each st (36)

R13: Working in FLO, 1 sc in each st (36)

Slst in the next st. Fasten off, and then weave in the ends with a tapestry needle. Place the eyes between R8 and R9, about 4 sc apart. Using black yarn, embroider the mouth onto the front of the face with a tapesty needle, just below the eyes. Add blush for rosy pink cheeks, if you'd like.

TEA

Using golden-brown yarn, join the yarn to the first back loop from R13 of the cup.

R1: [4 sc, 1 sc2tog] x6 (30)

R2: [3 sc, 1 dec] x6 (24)

R3: [2 sc, 1 dec] x6 (18)

R4: [1 sc, 1 dec] x6 (12)

R5: 6 dec (6)

Stuff the piece with polyester fiberfill.

Close off and then weave in the ends with a tapestry needle.

Cup, round 6

Cup, round 11

Tea, joining yarn

MiLLIE
the Milk Carton

There's such a sense of nostalgia around a good old-fashioned carton of milk. It reminds me of school lunches in the cafeteria, milk moustaches and leaving milk and cookies for Santa Claus. Well, Millie is here to bring back some of that childhood charm. Millie the Milk Carton is worked in continuous rounds and joins together seamlessly with no sewing necessary. We'll work three single crochets at each corner to create the base, then work our way to the top. Closing the top of the milk carton can be tricky; be sure to follow along with the photos. Millie's finished size is approximately 4 inches (10 cm) tall, 3 inches (8 cm) wide and 3 inches (8 cm) thick.

MILK CARTON

This piece starts at the bottom of the milk carton using white yarn.

R1: 4 sc in MR (4)

R2: 3 sc in each st (12)

R3: [2 sc, 3 sc in next] x4 (20)

R4: [4 sc, 3 sc in next] x4 (28)

R5: [6 sc, 3 sc in next] x4 (36)

R6: [8 sc, 3 sc in next] x4 (44)

R7: Working in BLO, 1 sc in each st (44)

R8–10: 1 sc in each st (44)

Change to light blue yarn.

R11–15: 1 sc in each st (44)

Milk carton, top alignment

(CONTINUED)

SKILL LEVEL

MATERIALS

1 oz white worsted weight/4-ply yarn

0.5 oz light blue worsted weight/ 4-ply yarn

Size E-4 (3.5 mm) crochet hook

Stitch markers

2 (6-mm) black plastic safety eyes

Scrap piece of black yarn for embroidery

Scrap piece of white yarn for embroidery

Polyester fiberfill

Tapestry needle

Cosmetic blush, for adding cheeks (optional)

TERMINOLOGY

R1:	row 1 or round 1
st(s):	stitch(es)
slst:	slip stitch
ch:	chain
sc:	single crochet
inc:	single crochet increase
dec:	invisible decrease
MR:	magic ring
BLO:	back loops only

Millie the Milk Carton (Continued)

Place the eyes between R9 and R10, about 4 sc apart. Using black yarn, embroider the mouth onto the front of the face with the tapestry needle, just below the eyes. Add blush for rosy pink cheeks, if you'd like.

Change to white yarn.

R16–17: 1 sc in each st (44)

R18: Working in BLO, 1 sc in each (44)

R19–23: 1 sc in each st (44)

Slst in the next st and fasten off. Stuff the piece with polyester fiberfill. Using white yarn, embroider the word "MILK" on the front of the carton with a tapestry needle.

Keeping in line with the base of the carton, place a stitch marker through the 2 stitches at each corner of R44 (there should be 9 sc between each stitch marker). Fold in the sides of the carton to shape the top. The folded ends should meet in the middle, with one stitch overlapping. The remaining front, folded and back stitches should line up. To hold its shape, place a stitch marker through all four of the stitches where they meet in the middle (see photo).

Using light blue yarn, join the yarn to the four stitches lined up on the right side of the piece. The next few steps are worked in rows instead of rounds.

R24: Working through all four stitches, 1 sc across (11)

R25–26: Ch 1, turn, 1 sc in each st (11)

Ch 1 then fasten off. Weave in the ends with a tapestry needle.

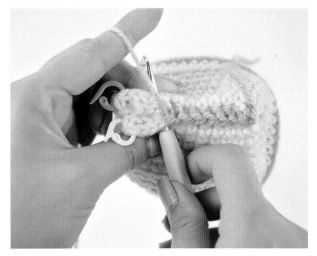

Milk carton, row 24

Millie the Milk Carton, finished

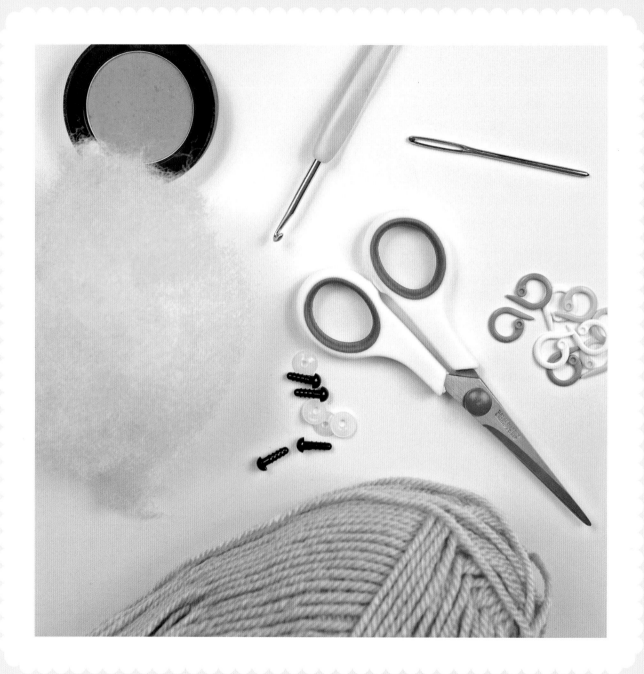

THE BASICS

One of the great things about amigurumi is that you don't need much to get started. There are just a few must-have items and one basic stitch. Once you've got those down, the possibilities are endless! In this chapter, I will go over the essentials, but there's always more than one way to get it done. Explore your own unique style and have fun!

If you are new to amigurumi, I recommend practicing some of the stitches and techniques until you are comfortable with the motions. It may feel awkward at first. But soon, you'll be able to crochet in your sleep!

TOOLS AND MATERIALS

These tools and materials are readily available in most craft stores or online. There are hundreds of variations, but they all function in more or less the same way. Try out different brands and styles to find what you like best.

Yarn: Acrylic worsted weight/aran yarn is my weapon of choice. It's inexpensive, durable and there are plenty of color options. Paintbox Yarns in Simply Aran is one of my favorites—beautifully soft and gorgeous color options. Red Heart's Super Saver is another great option and is available at most craft stores. When working through the patterns in this book, you can use any yarn material or thickness you like, just keep consistent throughout. Play around and see what you like best!

Hooks: I use an E-4 (3.5 mm) crochet hook with my worsted weight yarn, but feel free to figure out what works best for you. When you look at yarn labels, they will often provide a suggested hook size. For amigurumi, I recommend using hooks a size or two smaller to make sure your stitches are tight. I find that tight stitches create a cleaner look, help the piece hold shape and prevent any stuffing from poking through.

Safety Eyes: Safety eyes are available in different shapes and sizes to create unique looks. Just snap on the back washer to hold them in place. All the patterns in this book use 2 (6-mm) black plastic safety eyes, which can be found online.

Stuffing: Polyester fiberfill is available at most craft stores. Stuff generously, as the stuffing settles over time.

Tapestry Needle: This large, blunt-ended needle makes embroidery and finishing off a breeze.

Stitch Markers: When working in continuous rounds, it's easy to lose your spot. Use a stitch marker to mark the end of a round. As you complete each round, move the stitch marker up with you. If you don't have stitch markers, just use a scrap piece of yarn, paper clip or a safety pin.

Cosmetic Blush: Bright pink drugstore cosmetic blush works great. Just brush a little on either side of the face for rosy pink cheeks.

STITCHES AND TECHNIQUES

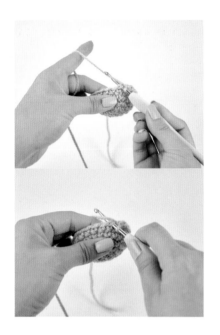

The two most common ways to hold a crochet hook are the "pencil grip" and the "knife grip." But, as long as the stitches work up correctly, there is no right or wrong way. Play around with what feels comfortable. With your other hand, hold the working piece between your thumb and middle finger. Drape the yarn over your index finger and through your hand to control tension. I typically like to use the "knife grip" in my right hand. Then with my left hand, I hold the working piece between my thumb and index finger while using my middle finger to manipulate the yarn. This isn't one of the more common techniques, but I find it works well for me!

One of the trickiest parts of crochet is making sense of all the terminology and abbreviations, but I will help you break it down! At the beginning of each pattern, I list all the stitches you need to know so you can quickly reference this chapter. As we work through a pattern, each line starts with the round/row number, the pattern instructions and the number of stitches completed in the round. For example, "R1: [2 sc, 1 inc] x6 (24)" means that for round 1, we work 1 single crochet in each of the next 2 stitches. Then we work 1 increase in the following stitch. The sequence between the brackets should be repeated a total of 6 times. By the end of this round, we will have completed 24 stitches. Gauge (how big your stitches are) is not particularly important so long as you are maintaining consistent tension in the yarn. If you make a mistake, no problem! Just remove your hook and pull the yarn end and the piece will unravel. Undo the piece until your mistake is gone, and then pick up where the pattern left off. Practice makes progress!

Slipknot: Make a loop around your first two fingers. The short end should be in front and the long end in back. Hold the yarn where the 2 strands meet. Insert the hook into the loop from front to back, pull the yarn through the loop, then tighten the knot.

Yarn Over (YO): Wrap the yarn over your hook from back to front.

Chain (ch): With a loop on your hook, YO and pull the yarn through the loop on the hook. When counting your chains, the loop on the hook is omitted.

Working in Rows: If you are beginning a new piece, start with a slipknot and then continue to create chains as specified in the pattern. When working into a chain, you typically begin with the second chain from the hook. To start the next row, the pattern will typically call for you to ch 1, turn and continue the work.

Working in Rounds: Amigurumi is typically crocheted in continuous rounds unless otherwise stated. No turning or joining needed. This creates a nice clean seamless look.

Front/Back Loops Only (FLO/BLO): The top of your stitches will look like a series of Vs. Insert your hook into both strands of the V unless the pattern states otherwise. But, when working in BLO, only insert the hook in the strand farthest from you. When working in FLO, only insert the hook into the strand closest to you.

Single Crochet (sc): This is the most common stitch in amigurumi. Insert your hook into the stitch or chain. YO and draw up a loop (pull yarn through st). You should have 2 loops on your hook. YO again and pull the yarn through both loops on the hook.

Increase (inc): Work 2 sc into the same st or ch.

Single Crochet 2 Together (sc2tog): Insert your hook into the st, YO and draw up a loop. Insert your hook into the next st, YO and draw up a loop. You should have 3 loops on your hook. YO again and pull the yarn through all 3 loops on the hook.

Invisible Decrease (dec): This can be used interchangeably with sc2tog. However, I prefer an invisible decrease when possible, as it creates a cleaner look. Insert your hook into the FLO of the first st, then insert your hook into the FLO of the next st. YO and draw up a loop. You should have 2 loops on your hook. YO again and pull the yarn through both loops on the hook.

Slip Stitch (slst): Insert your hook into the st, YO and pull the yarn through the st and the loop on your hook.

Half Double Crochet (hdc): YO, insert your hook into the st, then YO. Draw up a loop. You should have 3 loops on your hook. YO again and pull the yarn through all 3 loops on the hook.

Double Crochet (dc): YO, insert your hook into the st, YO and draw up a loop. You should have 3 loops on your hook. YO and pull the yarn through the first 2 loops on the hook. You should have 2 loops on your hook. YO again and pull the yarn through both loops on the hook.

Fasten Off: To fasten off, cut the yarn about 12 inches (30 cm) from your hook and pull the end through the last loop on the hook.

Close Off: To close off when working in rounds, cut the yarn, leaving a long tail, and pull the end through the last loop on the hook. Thread the end of the yarn onto a tapestry needle. Going clockwise through each stitch, insert the needle through the FLO, working from the center of the hole outward. Pull the yarn tight to close the hole.

For oblong pieces, use a whip stitch along the opening by inserting your hook from right to left through the first set of stitches. Then carry the yarn back over to the right side of the piece and repeat until the piece is closed.

Flatten and sc: To minimize sewing, many of the projects in this book require you to flatten and sc. Flatten the piece, ch1, and turn the piece so the yarn end is on the right. The front and back stitches should line up. Insert your hook into the set of front and back stitches closest to the hook and sc. Continue to sc through the front and back stitches until the piece is closed. Ch 1 and pull the end of the yarn through to fasten off.

Weave in Ends: For amigurumi, pull the end through the body and cut the excess yarn as close to the fabric as possible. The cut end will retract back inside the piece. For flat pieces, sew the end through several stitches and cut any excess yarn as close to the fabric as possible.

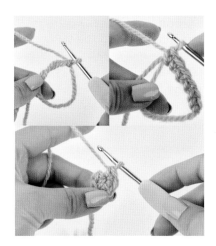

Magic Ring (MR): The magic ring (or magic circle) is a must for amigurumi. It creates a beautiful clean base to work with when crocheting in continuous rounds. To start, make a loop around your first two fingers. The short end should be in front and the long end in back. Hold the yarn where the 2 strands meet. Insert the hook into the loop from front to back, YO and draw up a loop, then ch 1. Continue to sc around the loop and yarn tail until you've completed the required amount, then pull the yarn tail to close the hole.

Join Yarn in Free Loops: Tie a slipknot at the end of the yarn. Insert your hook in the st, place the slipknot at the end of your hook, YO, draw up a loop and ch 1. This chain does not count as a stitch. Start your first stitch in the same stitch as the chain.

Single Crochet through Multiple Pieces: This technique is used to attach pieces without the guesswork of pinning and sewing. The add-on piece is worked into the main body by inserting your hook through the add-on piece and the main body together. Then YO to start your first sc. Continue to sc through both pieces until fully attached.

Change Colors: While still using the original color, stop when you have the last 2 loops on your hook. With the new color, YO and pull the yarn through both loops on the hook. Continue working with the new color. Cut the old color and tie the ends together inside the piece to secure.

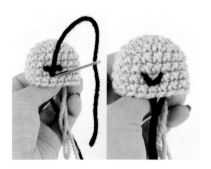

Embroidery: Embroidery stitches are often used to add details such as a mouth or eyes. Thread your yarn or embroidery thread on your tapestry needle. Starting from inside your piece, bring out your needle at one corner of the mouth and insert at the other corner. Bring out your needle in the middle, just below the corners (or higher for the eyes). Pull the needle through the loop and insert the needle at the same point to anchor the stitch. Tie the ends together inside the piece to secure.

Variations: There are countless ways to customize your designs. Instead of using plastic safety eyes, try embroidering your eyes or using buttons. Switch out your yarn for different colors and textures. Add a loop or keychain to the top and hang your creation. But most importantly, have fun!

SKILL LEVELS

Each pattern in this book is assigned a skill level between 1 and 5. Beginners are encouraged to start with level 1 projects and work their way up. But regardless of skill level, all the projects in this book are fun and unique in their own way. Even experienced crocheters may learn something new, but there are plenty of photos and details to help you along the way. For easy reference, I've organized the projects by skill level so you can develop your plan of attack!

Level 1

Level 2

Level 3

Level 4

Level 5

ACKNOWLEDGMENTS

I have to start by thanking Caitlin, who discovered my work, took a chance on a new author and guided me through the whole process. I'd also like to thank the rest of the Page Street Publishing team for transforming a bunch of scribbled notes stuffed in a drawer into a beautifully designed book.

A huge thank you to my fiancé, David. I never expected to take my business beyond just a few ready-made items on Etsy, but his endless support helped me to dream bigger and push myself as a maker. He let me commandeer the guest room for craft supplies. He put up with the constant hurricane of yarn and stuffing around the house. He even learned to crochet for me! How did I get so lucky?

Thank you to my pups, Carly and Duff, who somehow managed to resist destroying and eating all my designs. I am truly amazed and grateful!

I also want to thank Tiffany and Tanya for introducing me to amigurumi! None of this would have been possible without them.

Last, but certainly not least, thank you to my Mom and Dad for always nurturing my imagination and creativity as a child. It's easy to get caught up in academics and push arts aside. But they always encouraged and sometimes even forced me into music lessons, art classes and dance teams! Over the years, they have taught me about strength, independence, hard work and balance. I hope that I have made them proud.

ABOUT THE AUTHOR

Melanie Morita is the founder of the popular Etsy shop Knot Too Shabby Crochet. She began selling amigurumi plushes there in 2016, and she has also sold her work at a number of events and festivals.

INDEX